James Johnston

China and its Future

In the Light of the Antecedents of the Empire, its People, and....

James Johnston

China and its Future
In the Light of the Antecedents of the Empire, its People, and....

ISBN/EAN: 9783337166724

Printed in Europe, USA, Canada, Australia, Japan

Cover: Foto ©ninafisch / pixelio.de

More available books at **www.hansebooks.com**

CHINA AND ITS FUTURE

In the Light of the Antecedents of the
Empire, its People, and their
Institutions.

BY

JAMES JOHNSTON,
AUTHOR OF 'CHINA AND FORMOSA.'

WITH ILLUSTRATIONS.

LONDON:
ELLIOT STOCK, 62, PATERNOSTER ROW, E.C.
1899.

PREFACE.

THE present critical state of China, and the attitude of European Powers, compel me to issue at once this popular form of a work meant to be of more pretentious proportions, for which the materials were in a large measure prepared. If rapidity of production has, as I fear, left signs of haste in composition, I trust that, in the circumstances, good intentions will be an excuse for imperfect performance. No statement of fact has been made without good authority, nor opinion expressed without careful thought. There are some subjects on which there are repetitions in statement of facts or expressions of opinion, which are a fault in composition, but which I trust will be pardoned, if not approved of, on account of their importance in their bearing on the object of the work.

I do not rest my claim to be heard, regarding either the past or future of China, on a brief residence of a few years in that country—only long enough to impress a thoughtful student with the difficulties of the subject—but on a lifelong interest in Asiatic questions, especially those connected with China.

To one who has pored over the records of the history of China, covering a period of 4,000 or 5,000 years, and studied its institutions—the nearest, in a continuous and living form, to those of the earliest known inhabitants of our world—it is impossible to read with philosophic calmness the pretensions of the upstart nations of Europe to carve out for themselves, from that vast and venerable empire, provinces larger and with populations more numerous than their own territories and people—and that in the name of *civilization* of an empire which was civilized thousands of years before these nations had emerged from barbarisn.

While I admit the superiority of Western civilization in many of its aspects, I may ask, in the strong language of a distinguished American writer: Is China to be civilized by France, 'whose common sailors in a shipwreck clubbed drowning women and children who tried to get into the lifeboats? whose Parisian gentlemen trampled under foot the highest and best ladies in the land, leaving them to perish in the flames of a burning bazaar? and whose chivalrous generals condemn an innocent and brave companion in arms to the life and death of a felon, for the honour of the French army'? I may add, Is Germany to assist in this good work, whose merchants poison the natives of Africa with spirits fiery and noxious like turpentine? whose greatest statesman gloried in the acts of deception by which he raised his third-rate kingdom to a first-rate empire? and whose Emperor seizes a harbour and attempts to grasp a province of China as a solatium for the murder of a Christian missionary, while he claims as his dear friend the 'unspeakable Turk,' though his hands are dripping with the blood of thousands of Christians? Is Russia, only now in a state of transition from the serfdom or slavery of her subjects, and the use of the lash for the bare backs of women, persecuting and banishing Jews and Stundists at home, to aid in the civilization of China?—a land that has been singularly free from the spirit of religious persecution.

Even our own favoured country must wash her hands of all official connection with the opium trade, and do her best to arrest the evil it has inflicted on China. We must strive to undo the mischief caused by wars which have weakened the Government and disorganized the administration of the country—wars which the Christian politician can only defend by the use of what looks very like sophistry to soothe his conscience, which appears to the heathen a mere excuse for acts of high-handed cruelty and injustice. The most that can be said in their favour is that they were carried out in as honourable and merciful a spirit as was compatible with vigour and success—a spirit which was felt by the Chinese to be in striking contrast to their own internecine conflicts.

The fair, though favourable, description of the Chinese Empire is also designed to appeal to the just and generous sentiments of those who talk lightly of the partition of China among the Powers of Europe, as if it were the abode of barbarous tribes or of a bankrupt civilization. China is still capable of great things if the people are allowed fair play. They are only now awaking from the sleep of centuries. They are slow to move, but will have a momentum proportioned to their vast numbers. If broken up, they may inundate the lands of their conquerors with their swarming population, disorganizing the labour markets, and upsetting the costly enterprise of Western commerce by their industry, economy, and intelligence.

The destiny of China is committed by a higher Power as a sacred deposit to the keeping of Great Britain—the Power which first broke down the wall of exclusiveness, behind which the people had lived for untold ages in contented security and comparative comfort. I would earnestly appeal to the conscience of my fellow-countrymen to deal justly with a people whose future is in their hands; to their heart, that they may act generously toward a nation we have injured, while benefiting ourselves; to their imagination, that they may be tender in their treatment of an empire so ancient and venerable, and withal afflicted with not a few of the excusable infirmities of age, but still possessed of great recuperative power.

NOTE.

To any of our readers who desire to pursue the study of the subject, to which our small volume is an introduction, we would recommend such works as 'China in Transformation,' by A. K. Colquhoun ; 'Problems of the Far East,' by G. N. Curzon ; 'A Cycle of Cathay,' by Dr. Martin ; 'The Chinese and their Rebellions,' by T. T. Meadows ; 'Chinese Characteristics,' by A. H. Smith ; 'The Middle Kingdom,' by S. Wells Williams.

CONTENTS.

		PAGE
I.	THE COUNTRY	1
II.	THE PEOPLE AND THEIR PURSUITS	27
III.	THE POSITION OF WOMEN AND CHILDREN	51
IV.	THE HISTORY, GOVERNMENT, AND ADMINISTRATION OF THE CHINESE	62
V.	EDUCATION AND LITERATURE	92
VI.	THE RELIGION OF CHINA	127
VII.	THE FUTURE OF CHINA	150
	APPENDIX	173
	INDEX	179

LIST OF ILLUSTRATIONS.

	PAGE
PART OF A PASS IN THE LU MOUNTAINS, KIANG SI —2,300 STONE STEPS	*Frontispiece*
THE KULING VALLEY IN THE LU MOUNTAINS	8
KULING VALLEY	11
A TIGER TRAP	16
A WAYSIDE INN	24
FISHING WITH A NET FROM A PLATFORM	31
HEWING GRANITE	33
CLEANING COTTON	34
AN ITINERANT COBBLER	35
WEAVING AT HOME	38
THE RICE HARVEST	43
MOUNTAIN STREAM AND ARCHED BRIDGE IN FUH KIEN	68
UNDER- AND OVER-SHOT WHEELS	70
A MANDARIN REVIEWING ARCHERS	89
A SAMPLE OF A PROVINCIAL ARMY	112

CHAPTER I.

THE COUNTRY.

CHINA has an interest for every student of history, either sacred or profane, which no other empire, ancient or modern, can claim. It is unique in its extent, duration and isolation from the rest of the world. Modern empires have no past history like that of China, stretching away into the remotest antiquity. Ancient empires have disappeared, and we can only study them in uncertain traditions, or doubtful documents, or mouldering ruins; but China lives before our eyes, much the same as she was thousands of years ago. The existing empires of Europe are of yesterday, and can scarcely boast of as many centuries of dominion as the Chinese can of millenniums. Even the extinct empires of Greece and Rome are modern compared with the origin of the Chinese Empire. The ancient empires of Egypt and Babylon cannot claim an antiquity greater than that of China, while their dominion perished more than 2,000 years ago; but China, though old as they, still exists with

An interesting study.

an unbroken record of independent government—the oldest, the largest, the most populous, of any empire in the world, either ancient or modern.

Many names.

During its long history China has borne many names in foreign lands, none of them the same as that by which it designates itself. In ancient times it was called in the East *Sin,* or *Sinæ,* or *Seres,* or *Chin,* or, as in Isaiah, *Sinim;* and in the Middle Ages it was called by the Persian name of *Cathay,* or that by which it is still known in Russia, *Kitai.* The Chinese themselves from the twelfth century B.C. have called their country *Chung Koh,* or the *Middle Kingdom;* but other names have been used at different times, from the name of some powerful or favourite dynasty, such as *Tsin* in the second century B.C., imposed by the despot who united the small States into a united empire, and in later times after the illustrious Han dynasty. To this day the Chinese like to be called the *sons* or *men* of *Han.* In their pride they speak of their country as Thien Hia — All *under heaven;* or Sz Hai—All within the *four seas;* or in terms of affection they call it the *Flowery Land.* A recent writer in the 'Encyclopedia Britannica,' after a careful analysis of the opinions of the ancients regarding China under its many names, says: 'If we infuse into one the ancient nation of the Ceres and their country, omitting anomalous statements and manifest fables, the result will be something like the following—" The region of the Ceres is a vast and populous country, touching on

Ancient description of China.

the east the ocean and the limits of the habitable world, and extending west to Imaus and the confines of Bactria. The people are civilized, mild, just, and frugal, eschewing collisions with their neighbours, and shy even of close intercourse, but not averse to dispose of their own products, of which raw silk is the staple, but which includes also silk stuffs, fine furs, and iron of remarkable quality." That is manifestly a definition of the Chinese.'

'Comparing the description given above by the ancients with those of the Middle Ages, and with what we find them in our own day, we are struck with the marvellous uniformity which has existed for such a length of time. (The language of Ptolemy might be used in our day with perfect propriety, and) in the thirteenth century Carpini writes of them thus: "Now, these Kitai are heathen men, and have a written language of their own. . . . They seem, indeed, to be kindly and polished folks enough. They have no beards, and in character of countenance have a considerable resemblance to the Mongols, but are not so broad in the face. They have a peculiar language. Their betters as craftsmen, in every art practised by man, are not to be found in the whole world. Their country is very rich in corn, in wine, in gold, in silver, in silk, and in every kind of produce tending to the support of mankind." The notice of Rubruk, of the same period, shrewder and more graphic, runs thus: " Further on is great Cathay, which I take to be the country which was anciently called the land of the Ceres. For the best silk is still got from them. . . . The sea lies between it and India. These Cathayans are little fellows, speaking much through their noses, and, as is general with these Eastern people, their eyes are very narrow. . . . The common money of Cathay consists of pieces of cotton-paper, about a palm in length and breadth, on which certain lines are printed resembling the seal of Mangu Khan. They do their writing with a pencil such as painters use, and a single character of theirs comprehends several letters so as to form a word."'

Romantic fancies about China. Owing to its great extent and comparatively high civilization, China at a very early period took hold of the imagination of the world. The distance from the civilized nations of the West lent it enchantment, and a sense of mystery which increased its influence. Early writers expatiated on its grandeur and wealth, and described it as a spacious and happy valley surrounded by mountains; early travellers were ambitious to visit it, and traders were anxious to share its riches. It stimulated Columbus to reach its shores by a shorter and easier passage than by the overland route through Persia, and the inhospitable region of Tibet or the desert of Gobi. He tells us his object in sailing to the west, over unknown seas, was to reach 'Cathay and its outlying island of Zipangu,' or Japan, and now by the facilities of railway transit across the great continent which he discovered by mistake, a highway is opened up from Europe to China. That the ancients were not far wrong in their guesses about China is shown by the calm estimate of Sir George Staunton, one of the highest authorities we can quote. He says: 'Within an imperial ring-fence there is not, nor has there ever been, a country to be compared with China, in extent, fertility, and resources.'

More than a *fourth part of the human race* is contained within the limits of *China proper*, with a compact area of less than 1,400 miles in length and breadth. As has been said, you have only to cut off a few excrescences to make it a circle, or fill up a few corners to turn it into a square. We shall confine our description to what is called *China proper*, or the eighteen provinces. The four dependencies are Manchuria, the home of the present dynasty; Mongolia, the abode of a former foreign dynasty in China; and Tibet and Illi, conquered at different times, and retained under an easy form of subjection. They add immensely to the extent of territory, which with them makes the Chinese Empire nearly equal in area to those of Russia and England, while in population it is much greater than either; but they add little to the strength of the government, and less to its income. The climate of these dependencies is cold and inhospitable; the soil is barren, and fitted only for the rearing

<small>Extent and population.</small>

of sheep, cattle, and horses, by nomadic races in a low scale of civilization. The inhabitants of Mongolia and Manchuria despise the educated and civilized inhabitants of China as effeminate and timid, while the Chinaman looks down in contempt upon the unlettered and rude Tartar and Mongol. As for Tibet, it rears little except an unproductive race of priests and monks, whom the scanty lay population find it difficult to feed. These dependencies, from their poverty and constant struggle for existence, have never risen from a state of barbarism, and can scarcely be called a part of China, though Mongolia and Tartary have each founded a dynasty in the empire. But though military despots, the higher civilization of the conquered race subdued those of their conquerors who remained within its borders, while the rude races from which they spring are held as dependencies of China proper. China would have been better off without such neighbours.

Korea and Japan, the only external countries with which China had much intercourse, both borrowed their civilization and literature, and until recent times paid tribute as a token of allegiance and dependence. The area of China proper is seven times as great as that of France, and the population is ten times greater. Each of the eighteen provinces is, on an average, larger than England and Wales, and the population of the whole is thirteen times greater. China is equal to half the area of Europe, and contains more people. Its provinces are equal to the largest nations in Europe except Russia.

The resources of China are so great that its vast population of 400,000,000 can find all the necessaries and comforts of life within its borders. No other empire is so self-contained and independent of other countries, which accounts for its long isolation and its reluctance to trade with foreigners. It has no need for their products, and feels little desire to part with its own, for which there is abundant demand at home. Besides, those representatives of foreign nations who first sought commercial relations had acted so much like pirates or invaders that they and their countrymen were naturally looked on as barbarians, with whom intercourse was by no means desired by a civilized and peace-loving people. Since the character of a people, and their history as a nation, are largely influenced by the physical characteristics of the country they live in, we shall give a brief outline of the leading features of China. *Resources and independence.*

The geographical conformation of China proper is varied and interesting, and from its great fertility and boundless resources it can support its immense population. There are vast alluvial plains in the north, and rich fertile valleys scattered over the whole land; there is varied scenery of hill and dale in the east, and grand views amid the mountain ranges of the west and *Physical features.*

Rivers of China.

north. Its river systems are marvellously distributed. There are two rivers of the first class, the Yang-tze-Kiang and Hwang-ho, the former the third longest river in the world, and, if its tributaries be included, of far greater advantage to the country than its rivals, the Mississippi and Amazon, for irrigation, drainage, and inland

THE KULING VALLEY IN THE LU MOUNTAINS.

navigation. The Hwang-ho, which might under proper management be the source of unmeasured blessing, has by the neglect of the Government and its erratic course earned the name of 'China's sorrow'; but the glory of the Chinese riparian systems does not lie in the great length of the rivers, but in their number and distribution. The whole country is at once drained and fertilized by them, and no people have ever turned to account their water privileges as the Chinese have. They use them for transit all over the interior; they tap them for irrigation on every level plain, large or small; they drain them into canals, which again are made sources of irrigation and means of transit for the convenience of villages and farms, a double advantage to agriculture, for which our proposed light railways will be but half a substitute. These rivers of China *are her own*, great and small; their courses from fountain-head to their mouths on her own coasts are all within the limits of the compact but vast country.

The mountain ranges of China proper are to a great extent the continuation of those of Tibet and India. They stretch across the country chiefly from south-west to north-east, gradually diminishing in height as they leave the region of eternal snow in the Himalayas until they have only an elevation of a few hundred feet on the eastern shore. They send off many spurs to the north and south, besides which there are ranges of independent origin rising in different directions. The climate and rainfall are greatly modified by their distribution, much to the advantage of the country, which is, on the whole, healthful and well watered. *Mountains.*

The lakes of China are not numerous or large, but some of them are celebrated for their beauty, those of Hu-peh and Hu-nan being the chief. *Lakes and lake poets.*

The Tai Lake, studded with beautiful islands, is the paradise of Chinamen, and from time immemorial has produced its school of lake poets thousands of years before Wordsworth took up his abode on the shores of Grasmere. We quote from Huc's 'Chinese Empire' a poem of a later date by Sse-ma-Kouang, written about the end of the eleventh century of our era. With all the disadvantages of a translation, its appreciation of Nature is remarkable for the period, and worthy of one of the greatest statesmen of China. The closing sentences express no more than the sacrifice he actually made for his country. We have taken the liberty of turning the prose into blank verse, which claims no merit except fidelity to the translation:

'THE GARDEN OF SSE-MA-KOUANG.

' Their stately palaces let others build
To hide their cares, or to display their pride ;
Enough for me, a twenty acre plot,
To amuse my leisure, and converse with friends.
In midst of this a spacious hall I built
To hold my treasure of five thousand books.
In this I hold communion with the wise,
And talk with ancient sages in their works.
A small pavilion, built with modest taste,
Stands in the midst of water to the south,
Fed by a streamlet from the western hills,
Which plunges headlong from the mountain's side.
Here it has formed a basin, out of which
Five streams flow out like claws of spotted pard.
The graceful swans swim on its placid breast,
And in large numbers sport upon its banks.
On the border of the first, which plunges down
Frequent cascades, there overhangs a rock
Curved like the trunk of a huge elephant ;

The Country

Upon its summit stands a pleasure-house,
Where I can freely breathe the bracing air,
And see the rubies deck the rising sun.
The second branches into two canals,
Around which winds a double terraced walk,
Bordered with roses and with pomegranates.
The northern branch bends like the graceful bow,
And forms a little isle with sheltered bower,
Strewn round with sand and shells of varied hue ;
One half is planted out with evergreens,

KULING VALLEY.

On the other side the fishers' rude thatched huts ;
The other two seem to approach and shun
Each other playfully, as down the sloping meads,
Enamelled with gay flowers, they slowly glide,
Then leave their shallow beds to form small pools
Of purest pearl in emerald borders framed.
Anon they leave the meadows and descend ;
The waters dash against opposing rocks,
Fretting and foaming in their straitened beds,
Then rolling off in silver waves, they flow
Through winding channels, lengthening their course.

To north of the huge hall are sundry cots,
Scattered at random up and down the hills,
Nestling in narrow gorges half concealed.
The gravel pathways intersect the hills,
Shaded by tufted grooves of the bamboo,
So that the sun's fierce rays may not pass through.'

After a lengthened description of all parts of the garden and surrounding scenery, for which we cannot find space, and should only spoil by condensation, the poet goes on :

'When tired with writing and composing books,
I leave the hall and step into a boat,
In which I row myself from point to point
To seek fresh pleasures in my garden plot.
Sometimes I land upon the fishing isle,
Where with a broad straw hat upon my head,
To guard me from the sun's too ardent rays,
I wile the fishes with my tempting bait,
And muse on human passions like to theirs.
At other times, with quiver at my back,
And bow in hand, I climb the rugged rocks,
And thus like traitor lie, stealthily in wait,
Watching for conies creeping from their holes,
And with my fatal arrows pierce them through.
Alas! we men more foolish are than they;
They fly from danger, we do sport with it.

'The setting sun still finds me in my garden,
Watching in silence swallows in their flight,
Tenderly anxious for their little ones,
Or stratagems of hawks to catch their prey.
The moon arising gives an added joy;
The murmuring waters and the rustling leaves,
The beauty rare of heaven bright with stars,
Plunge me in rev'rie, speaking to my soul.
Wandering about I listen silently,
And night has reached the middle of its course
Ere I have reached the threshold of my door.

My learned friends sometimes invade my home
And listen to my works, or read me theirs,
Our frugal meal enlivened by good wine,
And seasoned by philosophy. At court

Men seek voluptuous pleasures, forging lies,
Fostering calumny, and laying snares;
While we're invoking Wisdom at her gates,
And offering her the homage of our hearts.
My eyes are constantly upon her set;
On me, alas! her rays come through thick clouds;
But let them be dispersed, though by a storm,
And then this solitude will be to me
The temple of felicity and truth.
What do I say? Shall I? A husband, father,
Citizen, and man of lettered fame—
My life is not my own, but to the State
By twice ten thousand duties I am bound.
Adieu, dear garden! once again, adieu!
Me love of kindred and of country claims,
The city calls me, and I must obey.
Then keep thy pleasures for some other day,
They may anon dispel some carking cares,
And save my virtue from temptation's snares.'

Few countries, if any, can boast of so rich and varied a flora as China. To give a long list of all the trees and plants that have been discovered on its soil would be a task tedious to the writer and unprofitable to the reader of these pages; but a few names of the more common and useful of the different kinds of plants may be interesting. *Flora of China.*

Of our own forest trees, the oak, the pine, the cedar, the chestnut, the willow, the thorn, and others, are found in abundance; of those strangers to our climate, the banyan extends its perennial shade over a vast area from its original root, with rootlets descending from its spreading branches—as much a village favourite as the oak and elm of our country. The camphor-tree grows to a large size, and the bread-fruit-tree with its blue blossoms is an attractive object; the betel-nut rises gracefully to the height of 50 feet; the rattan spreads its branches like the vine, and the variegated leaves of the castor-oil plant add beauty to the foreground.

There are few fruit-trees with which we are familiar in this country which are not found in China, such as the pear, the plum, the peach, and the fig, but they differ much in fruit and flavour from those of England. Of their own fruit-trees there is great variety and abundance. Their Chinese names would be meaningless; but those of the banana, the orange, the lime, the lychi, and pineapple are well known.

Vegetables of all kinds are abundant; we need only name melons, onions, leeks, cabbages, turnips, peas, beans, spinach, celery, and the sweet potato. The tea plant, by the cultivation of which China has laid the civilized world under obligation, introducing a cheering and refreshing beverage, comparatively free from abuse, is indigenous to the soil. It is a sad and humbling fact that we have repaid our obligations by introducing into that country the most seductive and pernicious of poisons—opium—a blight on the prosperity of China and the honour of England. But chief of all the productions of China is its rice, the staff of life to a Chinaman, who cannot conceive of people living without it. When he learns that rice won't grow in England, it at once explains to him why we are so willing to leave such a miserable country, and are so anxious to get access to China, where we can

A TIGER TRAP.

eat our fill of its choice food. The first invitation when a Chinaman meets a friend is, in the Amoy dialect, '*chia pung*,' 'eat rice.' It is equivalent to ' food.'

We cannot describe the flowers of China—so varied and abundant as to entitle it to assume the name of the Flowery Land. Many of those which grow wild in the fields and roadsides have been acclimatized as favourites in our own country. That queen of flowers, the rose, grows wild on the hillsides in China, along with the azalea and magnolia. The marigold grows by the footpaths, and the convolvulus covers large trees with its graceful flower and leaf; honeysuckle vies with it in luxuriance, and adds fragrance to its beauty, while violets and bluebells hide in the woodlands.

From the density of population and the high cultivation of the country, the fauna of China is limited, compared with its flora; there is more than enough of vermin, though even some of these are killed for food. In the north, bears are found, and would be more numerous, were it not that their paws are considered a delicacy of the table, which leads to their destruction. Deer and leopards are not numerous, and in the mountains around Amoy the royal tiger is sometimes killed, but unhappily is more frequently successful in this sport, at which two can play, by killing the natives. Of domestic animals the cat and dog are favourites in more senses than one; they are

The fauna.

not only prized as pets, but some species of dogs are more highly prized in the form of puppy-pies. Monkeys are found, and those in Shantung were said to have reached such a point of Darwinian evolution as to be employed in picking leaves from tea-plants that grew in precipitous places beyond the reach of human hands. Unfortunately for the theory, the tea-plant does not grow in Shantung. A few small oxen are reared in some parts, and the water-buffalo, with his subdued pessimistic look, is seen everywhere, dragging the plough or feeding in the ditches, often with his herd—a little boy—seated on his back and playing on a primitive Pan-pipe. Sheep and goats are scarce in most parts of the country, but the pig, being an economical feeder, forms the chief item in the rare animal food of the people.

Horses are small but hardy, like our Shetland ponies. Ignorance of this fact in natural history led to a ridiculous fiasco when Lord Macartney went in great state, with a magnificent retinue, as Ambassador to Peking in 1792. To make a great impression on the minds of the Emperor and his people, his lordship took out with him a grand state-coach, and, as he could not take his own large carriage horses, he took their gold-mounted harness and trappings, with his powdered coachman in state livery. The Emperor graciously promised to lend him horses, and did his best; but when the diminutive ponies in shaggy coats arrived, the coachman, who had never before sat behind such specimens of 'horseflesh,' rushed into his master's presence, and, in tones of horror, exclaimed, 'My Lord, *they have sent us four cats!*' The Ambassador had to content himself with a sedan-chair, followed by his powdered servants on foot.

China is as rich in treasures hid in the bowels of the earth as in the fertility of its soil, and can supply all her own wants out of her own mines. *All* the common minerals, except platinum, are not only found in samples, but produced at a price which shows they are abundant. Gold-mines are worked in the province of Shen-si, and the dependencies of Illi and Tibet, but gold is only used for ornament, not for currency. Silver is found in sixty-three different districts, and, along with copper, is the medium of exchange. Iron is found in abundance, and of the finest quality, and coal, that essential condition of power and progressive civilization, is found in each of the eighteen provinces of China. It is worked in seventy-four different districts. It is also found in the upper reaches of the Yang-tze-Kiang, cropping out of the face of the mountains through which the river has worn a passage. The mines are worked from a height of hundreds of feet above the bed of the river. The coal is lowered in baskets running on two thick ropes, like rails, stretched tightly at an incline to the river's bank. It can be bought 'at the pit,' at from about three to six shillings the ton.

<small>Mineral resources.</small>

These facts respecting the fertility and resources of that highly-favoured land account in a large measure for the early civilization of China, rendering it independent of external commerce, and have fostered the spirit of isolation and aversion to foreign intercourse. Their feelings have been strengthened by the rude manners and unrighteous conduct of the first foreigners who visited her shores. The Portuguese and Dutch acted like pirates, and our first English traders were little better, with their arrogant and blustering demands for trade, and their unprincipled smuggling of opium.

ABSENCE OF ARCHITECTURAL MONUMENTS.

Travellers frequently complain that the features of Chinese scenery are not adorned with castles and with stately mansions, like those of Europe, and that their old towns contain no venerable monuments of their ancient greatness, like the Pyramids of Egypt, nor remains of architectural beauty, like the public buildings of Rome, the temples and tombs of India, or the grand old cathedrals of Europe. It must be admitted that the Porcelain Tower,* the Great Wall, the Grand Canal, and a few second-rate temples and monasteries, are nearly all the works that can be pointed

* This famous tower was destroyed by the Tai-Ping rebels for *strategetic purposes*. It was supposed to render Nan-King impregnable by its favourable influence over the protecting spirits.

out. But is this to the credit or the disgrace of China? It is spoken of in a deprecatory tone by artistic travellers, who contrast this old civilization with the interesting ruins and splendid monuments of other lands.

To our mind, the absence of these old monuments from the cities and scenery of China is the highest proof of the superiority of China to these fallen empires of the West. For of what are the remains of these great works the proof? Look lower down than the outward show, and what do we find—beneath the display of genius in a few architects and engineers—but the evidence of tyranny, oppression and cruelty of the few over the many who were employed as slaves to turn the exquisite ideal of the brain into the material structure of stone? Strip them of the sense of awe and wonder with which we look on the Pyramids and Hindoo temples; get behind the sentiment of veneration and æsthetic feeling with which we gaze upon the ruins of Greece and Rome, and the mausoleums of the Mohammedan conquerors of India, and of what do we find them the price? The tears, groans and blood of a down-trodden, crushed and enslaved population!

The Pyramids of Egypt cost the prolonged misery and cruel oppression of millions of the people. It is said that 100,000 men were made to work three months in the year for eighteen years to build the Great Pyramid of Ghizeh, and that seems to have been constructed with the

Monuments Slavery.

least of oppression to the people of any. The Taj-ma-hall, the most exquisite work of art—'a poem in marble'—was the work of horrid cruelty; it was steeped in the blasted lives and cruel deaths of tens, if not hundreds, of thousands of innocent men, torn from their homes and families to rear a tomb to gratify the pride and soothe the feelings of a despot for the loss of one of his favourite wives. Thank God, China has no such monuments! Her kings never attempted such works as these, and the people were never such tools of despotism as to be thus enslaved and crushed.

What are even the great temples of India and the grand cathedrals of medieval Europe a proof of? We cannot help admiring their architectural magnificence, and we feel the sense of power or the soul of beauty so lovingly displayed in the genius and skill with which the wonderful effects are planned, and the minute care with which every detail has been worked out by master minds; but we cannot help reflecting on the painful fact that many of the grandest of these buildings, reared at infinite cost for the worship of the gods of India or the God of the Christian, were built through the spiritual tyranny—the most degrading of all forms of tyranny—of a despotic priesthood, working on the superstitious fears of a guilty conscience, by which the people were enslaved and oppressed. We are happy to say China never was deprived of religious liberty through the power of priestcraft, and the degradation of the people. These opinions will appear worthy of a Goth or Vandal, but a defence of the civilization of the most ancient empire in the world demanded their utterance, as an explanation of an admitted fact—the absence of æsthetic monuments in China.

It is characteristic of the Chinese people, and creditable to their common-sense and independence of spirit, that the only great monuments they can boast of are the Grand Canal and the Great Wall, both of them really great as engineering works, especially when we take into consideration the early date of their construction. The Great Wall was built by the Emperor Chi hwang ti 200 B.C., the man who reduced the many small independent kingdoms, which were at constant war among themselves, into one vast empire, and planned and extended this great work as a defence against the Tartar barbarians on the north, from whom it was for many centuries an effectual protection. It forms the northern boundary of China proper, and runs from east to west, across rivers, over lofty mountains, and through deep valleys, in an unbroken line of 1,255 miles. In its original form it was 20 feet high, 25 feet wide at the base, and 15 feet at the top, on which two chariots could pass with ease within the parapets; there are towers nearly twice the height of the walls at about every hundred yards of the entire length. Some idea of the greatness of this work may be gathered by a comparison with the famous Roman

The Great Wall.

24   China and its Future

Wall from the Tyne to the Solway, a distance of about sixty miles, built some 300 years later. The Chinese Wall, allowing for necessary deviations from the straight line, is 1,500 miles long, twenty-five times the length of the Roman Wall, besides being much higher and broader.

The Grand Canal. The Grand Canal, or 'River of floodgates' or 'locks,' as it is well called, is more characteristic

A WAYSIDE INN.

of Chinese peaceful industry, and their grand conception of commercial enterprise, than the Great Wall—a military scheme of the conqueror Tsin Chi, meant for the preservation of peace. By this canal, and taking advantage of rivers on its route, the chief cities on the north and south of China, Peking and Canton, were connected by unbroken water communication, and access obtained to the world outside by sea at the two extremities. This gave a stretch of 1,200 miles in what may be called a straight line. Of this water-way, between 600 and 700 miles are real canal, in many places 200 feet broad, and so laid down as to make it a highway to the capital from all parts of the Middle Kingdom by means of the rivers and smaller canals throughout the greater part of the empire. The commencement of the work is involved in remote obscurity, but it was completed by Kublai Khan, who deepened and extended it in the beginning of the thirteenth century, as we are told by the traveller Marco Polo, who resided at his Court and describes the work.

Such works as these are more worthy of a great and free people than Egyptian pyramids as tombs for the dead, Indian temples for the superstitions of the living, and Roman amphitheatres for the slaughter of men and beasts to amuse a cruel and depraved race.

INFLUENCE ON RELIGION.

The geographical features of China must have exerted an influence favourable to the maintenance of a moderate and rational form of religion, such as we find it. The blending of mountain and plain in due proportions under one race and one form of government saved it from the extremes

Physical geography and form of religion.

which a great preponderance of mountain or plain tend to develop. It never fell into the dark superstitions which characterize the religions of mountainous countries, with their fleeting clouds and raging tempests, which are supposed to indicate the fierce and malignant passions of the gods, nor did it come under the sensuous influence of the luxurious and sensual habits engendered by the wealth and ease of the dwellers in a fertile plain. The religion, like the social and political institutions of the country, developed itself into a mild and moral system very unlike those of their nearest neighbours, amidst the mountains of Tibet, on the one hand, and the soft inhabitants of India on the other.

CHAPTER II.

THE PEOPLE AND THEIR PURSUITS.

<small>Standard to measure by.</small> TO anyone who has lived in China, and has learned to know the people, and to feel a kindly interest in them for the good qualities which they do possess, it is painful to find in this country so strong a tendency to dwell on their faults, or turn their innocent peculiarities to ridicule. It is the custom of most to measure them by the high level of the Christian standard, and that, not of what we were even a hundred years ago, but by our attainments at the close of the present century, with all its humanizing influences. Let them be measured with the heathen nations of the present or former times, or even by what European nations were 300 years ago, and China will be found to compare favourably with the best of them, and greatly superior to any Asiatic people, ancient or modern. It is true they never attained to the literary or artistic excellence of Greece or Rome, but in the more important elements of moral culture their public standard has always been far higher than that of any heathen nation of ancient or modern times.

Characteristic qualities.

It is still more unreasonable to speak of the Chinese as objects of contemptuous ridicule because their manners and customs are different from ours. A clever traveller who has spent a month or two in the country, will tell, amidst the laughter of his audience, how the Chinaman wears a long pigtail hanging from the crown of his head, and will put his chief guest on his left hand as the place of honour, while he mounts his horse on the *off side;* how he actually writes from right to left of the page in lines running from the top to the bottom, and begins to read at the wrong end of a book; that he orders his servant to *whiten* his shoes, and wears *white* for mourning, while a dutiful son presents his father with a handsome *coffin* as a birthday present; how mothers bind the feet of their daughters until they can wear a shoe $2\frac{1}{2}$ inches in length, and poets indite verses, not to ladies' eyes, but to their little feet, which they call 'golden lilies,' and praise their graceful walk, which they declare to be as elegant as the waddling of a duck. One of our poets* tells the visitor to China that he will be waited on by smart young men about Canton in nankeen tights and peacock tails, handing you conserves of snails,

* The poet, if called in to cater for a Chinese dinner, would discover that 'the snail' was the rare and costly sea-slug or bêche-de-mer, and the 'bird's-nest soup,' instead of being found in every bush, was only found in some of the distant islands of the Malayan Archipelago, and was so scarce that good specimens would cost him 5 guineas the pound.

> 'With many rare and dreadful dainties :
> Kitten cutlets, puppy pies,
> Bird's-nest soup, which, so convenient,
> Every bush around supplies.'

We need not say it is folly to judge of a people by such superficial characteristics, exaggerated by poetic license, when the Chinaman can find as much to laugh at in our own habits and customs as we do in his. Of all nations, the Chinese are the last to be laughed at. They are a sensible, earnest, industrious, economical, hard-working people; their numbers, industries, commerce, literature, history, and character demand the respectful study of every thoughtful student. *Population.*

The population of China is one of the wonders of the world. That it numbers with its dependencies about 400,000,000 of people is allowed by the most competent judges. The Emperors of China had been in the habit of keeping a census of their people 2,000 years before such a thing was dreamt of in Europe; it was regarded as a sacred duty. The number of the people has been presented by the Emperor to Shang-ti (the Supreme Ruler) from time immemorial at the great annual sacrifice, with grateful thanks if there was an increase, and with lamentation and self-reproaches if there was a decrease in the population.

Deducting 20,000,000 for the dependencies would leave 380,000,000 for China proper, supported on a compact territory of 1,500,000 square miles, making about 280 to the square mile, a number not so great as that supported on many a *small* country like Belgium and England, but very great when spread over so large an area, including bare hills and the many barren regions which are inevitable in a country half as large as Europe, where the population is only on an average of ninety-one to the square mile, a third of the average over the whole of China. There is great diversity in the density of the population in different provinces. A large portion in the east and south has a population of only about 150 to the square mile, while the great plains on the north-east have an average of 450, and the province of Shantung has as many as 600 or 700 to the square mile. It would be unfair to compare provinces in China with European kingdoms in respect of density, for most of the latter are largely dependent on foreign countries for their food supplies. China, with a few exceptions, provides for her population from her own internal resources.*

How supported. But it may be asked, How can the land support so great a population? The answer is simple

. * Taking into account the habits of the people, there is nothing incredible in the numbers given. On the contrary, there is every appearance of probability of the numbers being accurate as given for each province. The fertility of each corresponds with the numbers assigned to it; 700 or 800 to the square mile is the largest proportion. Captain Wilkes found 1,000 people living on the square mile in the Fiji Islands, and 400 on half a square mile in an island of the Pelew Group, which are not more fertile than Kiang-Su and Ngan-Hwui.

The People and their Pursuits

enough. First of all, the people live almost entirely on vegetable diet and fish. To rear a sheep for food requires, we are told, as much land as would support a man, and an ox takes as much as would support eight men or two families. Then, the climate and soil admit of two

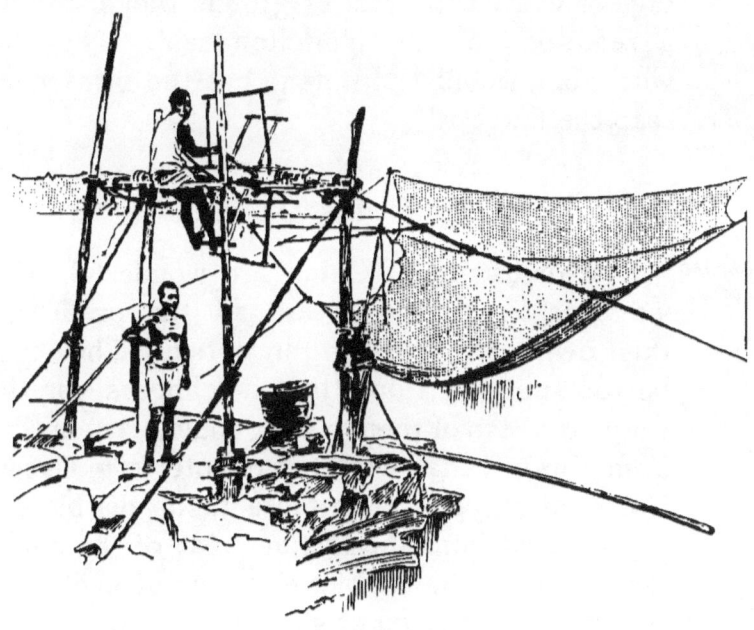

FISHING WITH A NET FROM A PLATFORM.

crops, sometimes three, to be grown on the same land in one year. Third, Chinamen reap a great harvest of fishes of all kinds from both sea and rivers. Shallow water on a flat shore or estuary is farmed for the breeding and rearing of fishes, as land is in this country for the breeding or rearing of sheep and oxen, and the rivers are kept stocked with fish, which are caught by all kinds of expedients. Fourth, the people are frugal, industrious, and excellent cultivators of the soil. Their system of rotation of crops and manuring and watering the soil is admirable. They turn everything to the best account, and take advantage of every little plot of ground they can plant a seed on; as Dr. Hamilton said, 'They sow where one would think none but the birds could reap the harvest.'

Industries and Arts.

Industries and arts. The industries of China are wonderful, when we consider that they are all the product of their own intelligence and invention. They could borrow nothing from their neighbours, for they were far ahead of them. They could learn nothing from Europe, they were too remote from Greece, Rome, or Egypt. It is more than possible that they carried from the original seat of the human race some of the simpler elements of civilization as they existed 4,000 or 5,000 years ago.

The arts and industries of China have an interest altogether their own. They have not only attained a high development: they bear their own evidence that they had reached the high position they now occupy at the very early date claimed for them in Chinese history, and confirmed by the independent testimony of early travellers, the ceramic manufactures, in which

The People and their Pursuits

China anticipated and excelled all other nations, giving the name of *china* to the finest forms of the work of the potter. The higher forms of that manufacture are now lost, and you may meet with Chinamen in every great European mart, where the finest antiquities in china-ware are on sale, buying the best of them at enormous

The older specimens the bets.

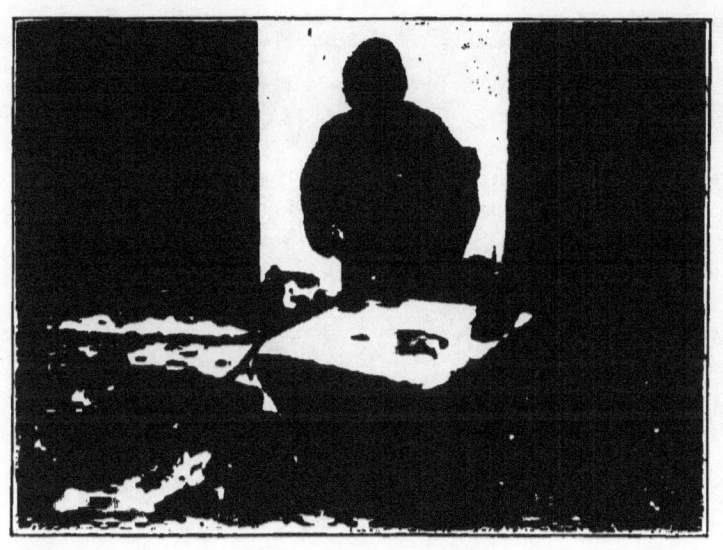

HEWING GRANITE.
(*By permission of Messrs. Newton and Co.*)

cost, to be taken back to China and sold at fabulous prices to the wealthy merchants and princes of their own country. Chinese collectors of bric-à-brac can boast of the finest specimens of their own *china-ware* as purchased in London, Paris, Vienna, or Moscow. It is much the same with their finest works in jewellery, wood, and ivory carving. The finest specimens are all old, and the next best are not new discoveries in art, but slavish imitations of the old. Even their manufactures in silk, for which they were the first to rear the worms, and to excel in weaving and embroidery, are only kept up by a careful imitation of the old styles and textures, even

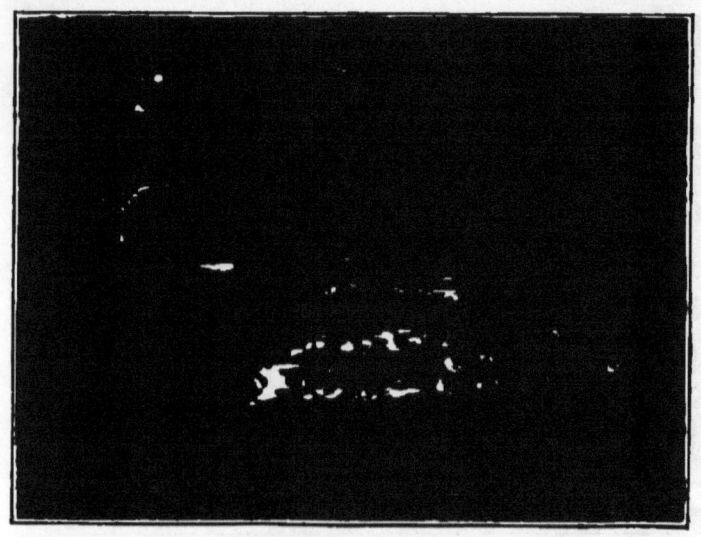

CLEANING COTTON.
(*By permission of Messrs. Newton and Co.*)

though as much encouragement is given to the silk trade as to agriculture. When the Emperor yearly ploughs three furrows in spring with his own imperial hand, and his courtiers a larger number, according to their descending ranks, the Empress at the same time goes out with her attendants to the mulberry groves, and feeds the

The People and their Pursuits 35

worms which spin the silk for the imperial offerings. All is done on the oldest methods, in the manufacture and in the ceremony; both are gone through to-day as they were performed by Yao and Shun 2,300 years before Christ.

In entering China for the first time, a visitor from the West is struck with the resemblance

Arrested progress.

AN ITINERANT COBBLER.
(*By permission of Messrs. Newton and Co.*)

of almost everything he sees, in its arts and industries, to what he has been accustomed to in his own country, but almost all in a ruder or simpler form, evidently old: the stunted form of an arrested growth is stamped on everything; and yet the people get on wonderfully with their primitive inventions. The lime-kilns on the hillside, the brick-works, in which the length, breadth, and depth of the bricks bear the same proportions that they do in this country. The carpenter, blacksmith, weaver, and ploughman go on using tools which bear the same resemblance to ours which the bud bears to the full-blown flower, all bearing the marks of a hoary antiquity. Paper, which was invented in China in the first century of our era, is still made in the same way. Printing from the written characters engraved on wooden blocks was discovered by Fung tau in the tenth century, and movable types were invented by a blacksmith of the name of Pi-Shing, in the year 1,000 A.D., 500 years before the discovery by Gutenberg, the supposed inventor, but never came into general use until the foreign missionaries perfected the system and used it first for printing dictionaries, the Scriptures, and other Christian books. The old types continued in use for printing some of the imperial edicts, and it is quite possible that Marco Polo may have seen them in the thirteenth century, and brought the invention to Europe. The habit of concealing new inventions, before patent laws were thought of, would account for China not getting credit for the discovery, and for the traveller not mentioning it.

Early inventions   There are many other useful discoveries of which we find the originals in China. The mariner's compass, at first called 'the south-pointing chariot,' was used in China about the commencement of the Christian era; and a dictionary published at that period describes the loadstone as 'that which gives polarity to the needle,' as good a definition as could well be given in this nineteenth century. It was first used for crossing the great deserts, but is now found in rude form, but well hung, in every fishing-boat on the coast. Gunpowder was invented in China 500 years before it was known in Europe, but was used for fireworks on occasions of rejoicing, and for firing salutes in honour of friends, not for the destruction of their enemies. It was Christians who taught them this form of civilization, in which they are still far behind their instructors.

TRADE AND COMMERCE.

The trade and foreign commerce of the Chinese can be traced back to the days of *Yao* and *Shun*. The great civil engineer *Yu*, who was employed by Yao for draining the water of a great flood, wrote an interesting book more than 2,200 years before Christ, called 'The Tribute of Yu,' the oldest book on commerce in the world, wherein he gives a list of the articles in which the Chinese of that time carried on trade with other nations. Amongst other things he names 'silk, lacquer-ware, furs, grass-cloth, salt, gems, gold, silver, and other metals, ivory, and manufactured goods.'*

Early trade and commerce.

* Williams, ' Middle Kingdom.'

The trade in these things seems to have been freer in Yu's time than under later dynasties, and it has not been much promoted by their present conquerors, the Tartars, until it was forced upon them at the cannon's mouth. Since then, foreign commerce has been greatly extended in tea and silks.

WEAVING AT HOME.

Home trade. The chief trade of China is within its own borders, which are large enough and sufficiently populous to develop the energies of the self-contained empire. Compared with this home trade, the external trade, large as it is, is of small value. So great is the home trade in tea and silk, that it is said the export trade has had no appreciable effect on the price of these commodities in

The People and their Pursuits 39

China. When tea and silk were exported to the value of £6,000,000 and £5,000,000 sterling a year respectively, it did not raise the price of tea one farthing in the pound to the nation, and the people of China did not pay a penny more for a yard of silk. The facilities for internal trade are good, and towns of any considerable size have their banks, by which letters of credit can be sent to any part of the country. Pawnbrokers' shops, which are numerous, and often very large, are said to have been the first banking establishments, and are still an important means for the transmission of money.

The number of cities in China is a sign of the commercial industries of the people; some of them are of great size, and count their inhabitants by millions. The provincial capital Wu-chang, on the south of the river Yang-tsze, with the cities of Han-yang and Hankow on the north of it, form an aggregate of population such as has never been collected within the same area in any other part of the world, except it be in London with its suburbs.

Cities in China.

The tendency to migrate from the country to the city was characteristic of the Chinese as a trading and commercial people from an early period. It may be that mutual protection was a factor in developing this tendency. It is said that there are no fewer than 1,700 walled cities in China, the walls of which would extend as much as 6,000 miles in length—a fourth part of the circumference of the globe. A good many of their cities contain more than half a million of inhabitants, and a few are much more populous. The confinement within walls has made narrow, ill-ventilated streets a general necessity, and, owing to the filthy habits of the people, they are generally malodorous and dingy. Some, however, can boast of large open spaces, with noble trees and wide streets, often ornamented with handsome monumental structures in wood or granite, elaborately carved or chiselled, to commemorate the virtues of distinguished men or women who have adorned the city by their lives, or by some special meritorious deed.

AGRICULTURE.

Agriculture honoured. It is characteristic of China that the tiller of the soil is held in public esteem as second only to the cultivator of literature. The Emperor and his highest officers of State, as we have seen, go through the form of holding the plough every spring as a religious ceremony, and an example to the people, and to impress them with the dignity and importance of agricultural labour. But important and honourable though it be, such is the supreme importance of literature, as laid down in the maxims and example of Confucius, that the cultivation of the mind comes before the cultivation of the soil in dignity and importance.

Tenure of land. The land of China belongs to the Emperor, as the father or representative of the people, and is rented directly from him by the farmers, though larger portions are held by the clans to which they belong, but with no trace of the feudal system. The clan may have a representative of its own, but his office is purely elective, and he has no personal claim on the land. The system is very much like the village communities which are still found in India, and have prevailed less or more over many parts of the world in the earlier stages of civilization. By Chinese law the lease of land is secured in perpetuity, in much the same way as it was secured to the Jews in Palestine by the laws of Moses. The man who has been registered in the Government office of his district as the tenant of land, and has taken what is called a 'red deed,' bearing direct imperial authority, cannot be legally deprived of it so long as he pays the rent, and in the event of its being mortgaged, he can at any time within thirty years get it back by payment of the mortgage. The forms of registration are simple, but the first expenses are comparatively heavy. These are evaded in case of transfer from one tenant to another by what are called 'white deeds,' binding the party to pay the land tax or rent. The rent of land, thus taking the form of an imperial tax, is not burdensome, amounting on an average to about six shillings per acre for good land, and from one shilling to two shillings or more for inferior soil. In the case of a tenant reclaiming waste land, he is allowed a number of years, less or more, according to the condition of the ground, free from rent or land-tax.

<small>System of farming.</small> The system of farming is rude but effective. More depends on hard labour than skill; but experience has taught many practical lessons, which the industrious farmer has not neglected. If his land is *light*, he dredges the bottom of the nearest river or canal to enrich it; if it is heavy soil, he dredges the sea for shells, which he burns to lime for his fields. To fertilize the fields, all kinds of vegetable refuse, with ashes, soot, bones ground to powder, hair shaved from the heads and beards of the millions of Chinamen, are carefully preserved and sold to the farmer, who collects every unclean thing from animals and men for manure. He has some notion of rotation of crops, and the system of farming is more like that of our gardener.

He hoes or digs the ground by hand labour, or, if the field is large, he ploughs it with the unequal yoke of an ox and ass, or, in some rude districts an ass is harnessed with his wife, the plough being little better than a converted hoe. The flooded rice or paddy field he ploughs with the water-buffalo, and in hilly regions he expends an amazing amount of labour in conveying manure, and even water, by human labour to the cultivated patches on the sides of the mountains. It takes all the patient and untiring industry of a Chinaman to make a modest living out of the small plots which they call farms. Though their occupation is honourable, the profits are small, and farmers are generally poor, but you occasionally come on larger farmers on rich soil, with all the air of respectability and comfort. Anything having the appearance of luxury or wealth is, however, carefully avoided, unless the owners be strong enough

THE RICE HARVEST.

to defy the attack of robbers, and the more oppressive exactions of the petty officers of the law.

It is computed, from very rough and unsatisfactory data, that the entire revenue from the landtax is from £15,000,000 to £20,000,000 a year. Of this only from £8,000,000 to £10,000,000 reaches the capital; the half of it is retained in the provinces for the support of the army and administrative purposes. The Central Government

Revenue from land.

derives large sums from a monopoly on salt and transit dues, so that, leaving out the last, the rent of land and profit on trade form the chief source of revenue, both land and salt being Government monopolies.

<small>Fossilized industries.</small> The peculiar feature of Chinese industries and arts is, as I have said, the absence of progressiveness. They reach a certain stage, and there they remain stationary, or if they change, it is for the worse. The cause of this lies in the educational, political and religious theories of the people. From the days of Confucius the principle has become fixed and unalterable that the only hope for the empire lies, not in progress or in the discovery of new truths and improved methods, but in *returning to the policy and practice of the ancients*, and the further back they can go the better for the people and empire. Yao and Shun, the first monarchs in their authentic history, were the models on which the education, politics and religion of the future were to be moulded.

Confucius was the perfect type of a conservative reformer, who could see nothing good in anything new. The whole tendency of his teaching was to fossilize all the institutions of the empire, and to bury them in the graves of Yao and Shun, who died about 1,800 years before his day. Do not let it be supposed that Confucius had any intention to oppose the scientific development of the arts and industries of his country. Science was undreamt of in his day, and such was the sage's

The People and their Pursuits 45

reverence for *truth*, we cannot conceive of him resisting light on any subjects brought before him. His successors have applied his maxims to subjects altogether beside the aim of his teaching. His reason for calling on kings and statesmen to go back to the days of Yao and Shun was that these men were the most perfect examples of pure, disinterested, and righteous rulers in the authentic history of the country. He meant no more than a Christian of our day who appeals to the example of Abraham as a model of obedience to the commands of God.

This tendency to degeneracy is the universal law under all heathen religions. Their best days are all in the past, and the consequence is they have *no future*, and no higher standard to which hope can aspire—hence the limit of their progress and consequent decay. Christianity alone looks to the future for its standard of attainment and perfection. It has every inducement to strive after a new and better state of things in a millennium of righteousness, peace and purity on earth, and a heaven of perfection and bliss beyond. Hope brightens the prospect, and faith is assured of a final victory over all the obstacles that oppose progress toward perfection in the individual or in the race.

False religions hinder progress.

This state of the mind in religion influences every department of secular life, domestic, social and political. It ennobles industry, elevates education as a means for perfecting the entire nature of man and all his works. The arts and sciences are inspired by higher aims, and cannot pause in their onward course. Even in the hands of secularists and agnostics the honest student breathes the bracing air of the Christian society in which he lives. Hope, like ozone, the unconscious tonic of our atmosphere, saves him from the despondency and pessimism which have led to decay and death in the heathen or godless systems of the past. We see the process at work before our eyes in the Chinese Empire, which will perish if it aims at a return to the days of Yao and Shun, but may be saved by accepting the better hopes inspired by the Christian faith and its fruits in the arts and industries of modern discovery.

Habits and Manners.

Civilized habits. On entering China from Western and Central Asia, the contrast between the habits and manners of the natives of these countries is very marked, and testifies to the superior civilization of the Chinese from an early period to the present day. Their life in the open air, or with open doors, gives ample opportunity of forming an opinion. In Arabia, Ceylon, India, and the Straits of Malacca, you see the poor sitting on the ground or the floor of their huts eating their food with their fingers, often sitting round the same bowl, and all dipping into the same dish. The rich

The People and their Pursuits 47

only differ by having mats or cushions to sit on, and greater facilities for washing their hands while eating in the same primitive fashion. In China the poorest beggar would not think of touching his food with his hands, and every man has a seat of some kind, from the bamboo stool of the poor to the elaborate carved chair of the rich. Each has his spoon and his chopsticks, which may be awkward to the amateur, but at least have the merit of being cleanly, and a decided advance on the habits of monkeys and kangaroos.

The sleeping arrangements of the Chinese also show a great superiority over those of other Asiatic nations. Instead of lying down on mats or cushions spread on the floor, as is the custom of even the civilized nations of the East, the Chinese for the last 4,000 years have slept on beds of some kind; it might be only a board or cane frame on trestles for the poor, while the rich have slept on four-post beds, with silk or satin curtains, from before the Christian era.

Asiatics are generally polite even to servility, but the Chinese have elevated politeness into a ritual, tedious and wearisome to an impatient European, but to the leisurely Asiatic sacred and important as a religious duty. Sages in China have devoted their attention to the regulation of the forms of social intercourse, on the principle that the outward forms of courtesy are essential to the cultivation of the feelings of respect and

Manners and customs.

affection, of which they are the natural expressions. The 'Book of Rites,' which treats chiefly of forms and ceremonies for all occasions sacred and secular, from the highest formalities of the Court and the altar down to the humblest duties of the meanest subjects in the ordinary courtesies of daily life, is one of the most ancient and sacred of the classics. In its original form it was attributed to Confucius, but only as editor or 'transmitter.' The substance of its teaching is traced back to a period 2,300 years before Christ. It gives the minutest details of the duties to be performed to God and man, and of the forms to be gone through, of the dresses to be worn, and even of the manner and expression of the countenance in which the ceremonies are to be performed. The daily forms prescribed for a married son and the younger branches of the family in serving their parents will give some idea of the attentions prescribed in this 'Book of Rites.' It says:

Duties of children. 'Men on serving their parents at the first cock-crowing must wash their hands; rinse their mouths; comb their hair; bind it together with a net; fasten it with a bodkin, forming it into a tuft; brush off the dust; put on the hat, tying the strings, ornamented with tassels; also the waistcoat, frock, and girdle, with the note-sticks placed in it, and the indispensables attached on the right and left; bind on the guards; and put on the shoes, tying up the strings.' The wife being dressed with equal care, 'they then go to the chambers of their father and mother, and father-in-law and mother-in-law, and having entered, in a low and placid tone, they must inquire whether their covering is too warm or too cold, and ask if they are free from pain and discomfort. In bringing the apparatus for washing, the younger (if there are other sons) must present the bowl, the elder the water, begging them to pour and wash, and after they have washed hand them the towel. In asking, and respectfully presenting what they wish to eat, they must cheer them by their mild manner, and must wait until their father and mother, and father-in-law and mother-in-law, have eaten, and then retire.'

The duties in every relation of life are laid down with like minuteness of detail. The following advice for conduct at the table, quoted by Abbé Grosier, from one of the classics, at least 500 years before Christ, is worthy of that accomplished exquisite of the eighteenth century, Lord Chesterfield: *Manners at table.*

'When you entertain anyone, or eat at his table, pay the strictest attention to propriety; be careful not to devour your victuals greedily; never drink long draughts; avoid making a noise with your mouth or teeth, and neither gnaw your bones nor throw them to the dogs; never sop up the broth that is left when everyone else is done, nor testify, by external signs, the pleasure you receive from any particular food or wine; neither pick your teeth, blow upon wine which is too warm, nor make a new sauce to whatever is placed before you; take small bits at a time; chew your victuals well, and never let your mouth be too full.'

Forms useful. Chinese ceremonial prescriptions appear to us too elaborate and minute, but if we look back to the long history of this great empire—the longest and largest which has ever existed in freedom and independence, with so large a measure of peace and prosperity—we are constrained to admit that its laws and customs must have been suited to the character and circumstances of the people. To us they seem fitted only to produce a race of formalists or hypocrites. To them they appear to have kept up the spirit of reverence for parents which has been the basis of loyalty to the Emperor, the father of the people, and the security for peaceful submission to 'the powers that be.'

CHAPTER III.

THE POSITION OF WOMEN AND CHILDREN.

The place of women.

THE character of a people is largely formed by its mothers, and we may judge of a nation's character by the place that women occupy in its social and domestic circles. The treatment of women in China varies not only with their social position, but with the parts of the country in which they live. With all its apparent sameness, China is not homogeneous; there are marked differences in personal appearance, character, and customs of the people, and with all its apparent stereotyped fixity, it has varied much in its habits during the long period of its history.

In early times women seem to have occupied a better position, and were not so far removed from equality with men as they now are. By the time of Confucius they seem to have reached much the same level as they now occupy, and from the wide influence of his writings all over the country the differences are not very material. When once the woman has attained the position of a mother of sons, she rises much in the scale of popular esteem; but if only of girls, she falls lower than ever. When once she becomes, by the death of her husband, the female head of the family, her power over sons, daughters-in-law, and grandchildren is despotic. The want of education is at once the result of the low place that woman occupies, and tends to keep her low. There have been learned ladies in China, but their number was never large, and now it is very small.

<small>The mother of Mencius.</small> The praises of good and wise women are recorded in history, and illustrated by monuments in the principal streets of their cities. One of the best was the mother of one of the most distinguished philosophers of China, Mencius. She was left a widow with this one boy, and on his account twice changed her abode. In the first, which was opposite a cemetery, her little boy began to amuse himself by imitating the funeral rites; so, lest he should lose reverence for the dead and sympathy with mourners, she left the locality. The next house was opposite a butcher, whereupon her son took to killing toy lambs for his amusement. Again she left her house, lest her boy should become cruel. In the third choice she was more fortunate: it was opposite a school, and her son began to imitate the boys at their lessons, and became a famous scholar.

Women in China have occupied places of power in many departments. They have been distinguished as Empresses, of whom the present Dowager-Empress is a striking example. Chinese women have led armies, have been distinguished poets, and leaders in philanthropy, and one scoured the sea as a pirate. These are rare examples, but they show of what they are capable, and inspire the hope of their rising to the high position of true womanhood, when they are released from their present degradation and sordid drudgery by education and equality of privilege with the men. They never have sunk so low as women in Hindoo and Mohammedan lands, and their elevation will be all the easier and more speedy.

The marriage customs of the Chinese vary with the habits, conditions and locality of the wide empire. The general rule is monogamy, according to God's original plan, as delivered in His Word, and indicated to the heathen by the practical equality in the number of the sexes. There are, however, exceptions, in case of there being no son to perform the funeral rites, in which case a second marriage is not only lawful, but is looked upon as a religious necessity for the well-being of the souls of both husband and wife. It is then that a false religion becomes a cause of both sin and misery to its professors; the second wife occupies an inferior place, or may be only a concubine and little better than a slave, like Hagar in the family of Abraham. In the case of rich men, there is a great deal of license in adding both secondary wives and concubines to their domestic troubles. That polygamy is lawful *Marriage.*

there can be no doubt, and the example of the great Emperor Shun can be quoted. That pattern of propriety gave two of his daughters to Yu 500 years before Laban imposed his two daughters on poor Jacob. In some parts of the empire the marriage bonds are very lax, especially among the aboriginal tribes, and polyandry prevails in Tibet.

Prohibited degrees. The *prohibited degrees* in China are peculiar. By both law and custom, no man or woman can marry anyone of the same family name, however numerous the owners of the name may be—often a large and powerful clan. The law seems to have been formed with a view to put an end to clan feuds, or to mitigate their severity. In spite of that law, these feuds are a source of much mischief, but they might have been worse had it not been in operation.

Divorce. Divorce is too costly an indulgence to be practised by the poor, and is not common among the rich. True, there are *seven* grounds on which a Chinaman can lawfully put away his wife; these are barrenness, talkativeness, thievishness, disobedience to her husband's parents, leprosy, jealousy, and lust. But these many sanctions for divorce are practically nullified by the merciful condition laid down by the law, that no man can send away his wife for one or all of these seven reasons *unless her parents are living to give her a home*. In case of adultery, the law not only sanctions the death of the guilty wife, but compels the husband to put her to death.

The Position of Women and Children

There is one cruel custom which is not legal, but which is not taken notice of unless the relations of the woman interpose: a man may put his wife to death in his own house if he can get her mother's consent to do so. A lady who has worked for years among the women of Southern China writes :

'A man may even kill his wife; providing her own relations do not take the matter up, no notice is taken of it. A woman whom I know well, and who is still living, was nearly put to death by her husband because she had become a Christian. Her mother gave the husband and his family permission to put her to death. He proceeded to do so—had her hung up, hands and feet tied by a rope to the ceiling. When nearly dead, the mother's heart relented, and she bade them stop, a request they dare not disobey, so she still lives to tell the tale.'

The preliminaries of marriage are tedious, and are all carried on by second parties. The go-between is an important personage, and plays the principal part. It is only through her eyes that the bridegroom sees the bride, and as the girl's parents frequently bribe her to look at their daughter through golden spectacles, the most deformed and unsightly are described in the most glowing colours. 'To lie like a go-between' is a common saying in China, and yet, such is the tyranny of custom, parents and young men will trust them in the most important transactions of

Marriage customs.

life, and never see the bride until she is brought home for good and aye, often leading to grievous disappointment and lifelong misery. The disappointment is frequently as great or greater on the part of the bride, and often leads to her committing suicide. Even if the husband prove all the bride could wish, she may be kept in a state of constant degradation and misery by a cruel stepmother, to whom she must yield absolute submission and pay the highest honour, whatever her character may be.

<small>Happy marriages.</small> But let it not be supposed that all marriages in China are unhappy; there are fine examples of domestic happiness amongst both rich and poor. Women in China, from centuries of subjection, are humble in their expectations of happiness, and put up with much which would destroy the happiness of a Christian home. They do not expect to be treated as the equal of man. The wife never would think of sitting down to a meal along with her husband. They do not even object to a reasonable amount of physical correction. One of the questions constantly put by Chinawomen to English lady visitors is : ' Does your husband beat you ?' And the expression of amazement at the emphatic ' Never !' is a painful evidence of the frequency of such chastisement among themselves. We need not, however, boast of our immunity from this relic of barbarism. It is not so long since English husbands abandoned this privilege, for we have heard the right was

legal, provided the stick with which he beat his wife was not thicker than her thumb. We are told by Sir Walter Scott that ladies, even in chivalrous times, preferred a husband who beat them, provided he showed his valour by more soundly beating his enemies. Unhappily, this old vice of wife-beating has not quite died out, even in happy England.

Another evil, which is almost universal in the East, prevails in China—the custom of sons remaining after marriage in the paternal home—so that two or three generations are found huddled together under one roof, or in houses built so closely together as to form one community under the despotic government of the grandfather or grandmother.

From this arrangement of one family and one purse, with so many diverse interests, managed by even patriarchal despotism, the preservation of harmony is rare, and constantly liable to be turned to discord. The power of one evil-disposed member of such a group of discordant elements will destroy the peace of all the household, as one false note in the best of music will spoil the finest harmony. A true *home*, in the English sense of the word, is almost impossible.

A redeeming feature in the position of woman in China is the respect she receives from her sons, especially after they are grown up. From the time she becomes the mother of a son her social and domestic position is secured, and as the

The redeeming of womanhood.

number of sons increases, she rises higher and higher in the social scale, and receives an amount of respect which might well satisfy a European mother ; and in old age, when her sons are settled around her with their families, she becomes the centre of an obedient and respectful circle of children and grandchildren. This reacts on the character of the woman, and keeps up the ideal of womanhood in both sexes. The power of such a mother is very great. Neither sons nor daughters dare to resist her authority. She may, according to Chinese custom, not only demand obedience, but enforce it with sharp blows on the shoulders of sons or daughters or grandchildren. For one to resent, or even threaten to return, her blows would expose the offender to the penalty of death by Chinese law. This possession of supreme authority in the family circle has done much to redeem womanhood from degradation. We have often admired the quiet and dignified bearing of these old matrons, and have thanked God that China had such mothers, not only for the sake of womanhood, but for the sake of the manhood of the country. This dignified position of the old goes far to save from despondency or despair the younger women of China. The prospect of attaining to such a position inspires hope amid their many trials and sufferings in youth.

Children.

Filial obedience. That which is China's greatest boast—the devotion of children to their parents—is a source of perplexity to casual observers. They see that boys show little or no respect to their parents in daily life—in fact, they are petted and spoiled, and as a natural consequence are disobedient and disrespectful; but the curious circumstance is that as they grow up they do become, as a rule, obedient and even affectionate—at least, in outward appearance. It seems as if the atmosphere of Confucian influence in the teaching of the schools and in the intercourse of daily life moulds them into the form of what has for thousands of years been the constitutional habit of the people, and has been the preserving salt in the moral and political life of the nation.

One of the most pleasant sights in China is the number of old and venerable men and women to be seen in the villages, the men sitting under the shade of the spreading banyan-trees, and the old women at the doors of the houses, enjoying the ease and comforts of age supplied by the industry of the children and grandchildren. It is rare for a son to neglect his duty to his parents either in old age or after death. The public sentiment on the subject is so strong that the man who would run counter to it would need to be a bold as well as a bad man. Even amongst

the most lawless class the feeling is powerful.
There was a striking instance of this just before
we arrived in China. A local insurrection had
been suppressed, but the ringleader had escaped,
and was safe among a band of pirates—the most
ruthless class in China. The authorities had,
however, got hold of the father, who by Chinese
law is responsible for the crimes of his children.
They sent word to the son that if he did not give
himself up to justice, which meant certain and
cruel death, they would punish his father in his
place. The man, rebel and pirate though he was,
sent back word that he would surrender himself if
they would ' promise to send him to his ancestors
with his head on' (the Chinese have a great aversion to decapitation). They agreed to the terms.
He gave himself up, and *was buried alive*. He
would have been an object of contempt even
amongst pirates if he had refused to save his
father's life at the expense of his own.

Education of children. The number of boys who receive a literary
education is very small, and of girls practically
none. The number who are taught to read and
write is so few that they only form the exception
which confirms the rule. But a large number of
boys get such a knowledge of writing and arith-
metic as enables them to keep their own accounts
when in business or to find employment as clerks.
The strange thing is that, while they are ready
with their pen or pencil, and quick and accurate

The Position of Women and Children

in their calculation of sums, they cannot read the simplest book on any subject.

There is, however, one important element in Chinese education which has had a powerful influence in the formation of the character of the people: every child is carefully drilled in the performance of domestic and social duty. The forms and customs taught have a moral element. Confucius always made the outward form the expression of inner feeling. But, best of all, the influence for the formation of character in Chinese education is the purity of their school-books. The moral element is wholesome, and no book would be tolerated in China which contained such passages as are found in the Greek and Latin classics. As for the stories of the gods told in Indian native schools, and which the teachers (often priests) gloat over and present in their most realistic impurities, they would be rejected with horror by every teacher in China. This purity of Chinese school-books and classic literature has done much to preserve a fairly sound conscience and wholesome public sentiment in China.

CHAPTER IV.

THE HISTORY, GOVERNMENT, AND ADMINISTRATION OF THE CHINESE.

History.

Chinese 'historic sense.'

THE Chinese have shown an amount of common-sense and of historical insight rare amongst Asiatics. In a country like India it is almost impossible to draw the line between history and myth; and if a line is drawn, the improbable or impossible is preferred to commonplace facts. In China the historical spirit prevails, and has prevailed from time immemorial, and the Chinese show their caution and critical spirit by treating the times of Fuh-hi, who is said to have flourished about 3,300 years before Christ, as legendary or doubtful. There are stories of long periods prior to this, which are treated as myths by historical writers, who say that they are the product of the imaginations of their later philosophers, who *invented these long periods to allow of time for the development of their theory of the production of all things from the principles of the Yang and Yin.*

which may be loosely rendered the *Male* and the *Female*, or the *active* and *passive* powers of Nature, by which all things in heaven and earth were produced. This process required endless ages for its operation, as Evolution does in modern theories. Chinese historians seem to show an excess of caution when they treat the period subsequent to Fuh-hi as legendary, for there is good ground for accepting the accounts of his reign as authentic. He is generally said to have begun to reign 2852 B.C., but Dr. Legge gives good reason for placing it 500 years earlier, in 3322. This date is rendered the more credible from the discovery of Accadian and Egyptian records, which seem to carry authentic history back to a point about 400 years earlier. The philosophers of China, reasoning about causation, claimed time for the operations of the *Yin and the Yang* to construct a cosmogony, the origin of which carried things back to 45,000 or 50,000 years before Fuh-hi. They were modest in their demands when we consider that heaven and earth, and all things in them, had to be fashioned. Scientists of our day demand 20,000,000. All the *heavy work* seems to have fallen to Pwan-ku, who fashioned the earth, and scooped out the heavens with his great chisel and hammer. He was himself produced from chaos, and as he added six feet to his stature every day, and continued his labours for 18,000 years, he was able to reach high enough without a ladder before his work was finished.

Excess of caution.

Authentic documentary history in China, beginning with the reign of Yao in 2356 B.C., synchronizes with the authentic histories of Chaldæa and Egypt, both of which are now generally said to begin about 2,200 or 2,300 years before the Christian era, though some carry a few scraps of history 1,500 years further back, as Chinese scholars do that of China.

<small>Twenty-six rebellions, one revolution.</small> There is a general impression that Chinese history is a dead level of uninteresting monotony. If it is so, it is the fault of historians. The materials for history are full of life and tragedy; it has not enjoyed that unchanging peace which makes history dull. The Chinese Empire can make the very doubtful boast of having survived twenty-six successful rebellions, leading to as many changes of dynasty, besides an unknown number of unsuccessful ones, quenched in blood sufficient to satisfy the vulgar taste of modern novelists, not to say of historians. All the successful rebellions were, according to Chinese theory and European practice, justified by the approval of Heaven. Of these twenty-six rebellions only one could be called a revolution —that of Chi, the Napoleon of China, who reigned 250 years before Christ. He was the first to subdue all the smaller kingdoms into which the country had formerly been divided (like our Heptarchy on a small scale), and to establish the one great empire which it has ever since remained, a monument of military genius and political sagacity.

The History of the Chinese

It was he who built that one great wonder of an architectural kind of which China can boast—the Great Wall—to defend the country from the invasions of the Tartar hordes on the north, and he and his successors drove the Huns from his western border, and compelled them to seek easier conquests in Europe. There were constant wars carried on against the wandering tribes on the north and west until Illi, Mongolia, and Manchuria were added to the empire, and Tibet reduced to a dependency. On the east war was carried by the navies of China into Corea and Japan, both of which were made tributary, and remained so until quite recent times. The Mongol and Manchu invasions were successfully resisted until the end of the thirteenth century, when the former power gained possession of the throne, but was expelled in 1368 by the peasant patriot whose dynasty continued until 1644, when the present Manchu dynasty established itself on the throne of China.

Even the successive conquests of China by the Mongols and Manchus caused no revolution in the government of the country. They either recognised the Chinese laws and administration to be superior to their own, or did not feel strong enough to interfere with what was held so sacred by the millions of the peaceable inhabitants of the country they had conquered by military skill and courage, though so inferior in numbers. With the exception of these two foreign conquests, all

Invasions not revolutions.

the internal rebellions were carried to a successful issue on old lines, and with the avowed purpose of restoring the laws and usage of Yao and Shun, the model rulers of antiquity. Both of these rulers showed their patriotism by passing over their own sons, and nominating the most competent men in the empire as their successors to the throne.

Origin of the empire. It is difficult—perhaps impossible—to trace the early history and development of an empire which can claim an origin so remote as that of China. It has been supposed, on what seems good evidence, adduced by Dr. Legge, that the founders of the empire entered China from the north-west —a nomadic race which had at a very early period broken off from the original home of the human family in Western Asia to the south of the Caspian Sea, and settled in the upper reaches of the Hwang-ho, where they mingled with some of the original inhabitants, and drove others into mountain fastnesses. They gradually overspread the country, and founded a number of separate States, which were eventually merged into one great Chin dynasty by Chi 200 years before Christ. The form of the roofs of the houses, with their tent-like sweep, suggests a nomadic origin. To the present day builders are in the habit of erecting the roof of their one-story houses first, resting it on pillars, and building the walls under them. When the Tartars, who preferred the tent to the house, conquered China, they pulled down the walls, and dwelt under the roofs.

It appears from the early histories of China, that whoever they were, or from whatever quarter they came, the first settlers of the present inhabitants were far from being a barbarous people. They brought with them the elements of civilization, much superior to that of the aborigines, which formed the basis of all their future progress. They brought the art of writing with them. It is incidentally mentioned that they presented a written petition to their King in the eighteenth century before Christ. From these early times— about 4,000 years ago—on to the appearance of Confucius, 500 years before Christ, the records are too imperfect to allow of a satisfactory account of the development of the industries of the people and the institutions of the country. From that time the records seem to be too full for any European historian to systematize or reduce to a readable compass. *Early civilization.*

Yao, although he reigned 2,300 years before the Christian era, was not by any means the first ruler in China. His reign was that of an advanced civilization, when the people were clad in garments of wool and silk robes of varied colours, richly embroidered, and when the arts and manufactures, and even external commerce, were carried on with the petty States, but chiefly within the limits of what was then the Empire of China proper. His successor, Shun, is represented as carrying on extensive engineering works, which some pious students of Chinese history have taken to be the *Early history of China.*

China and its Future

draining off of Noah's flood, but which is much more likely to have been a flood caused by that great river, the Hwang-ho, changing its course, as it has repeatedly done, devastating whole provinces.

The engineer Yu. His engineer was the great Yu, who forced the river back to its old channel and drained the

MOUNTAIN STREAM AND ARCHED BRIDGE IN FUH KIEN.

flooded plains. It took him nine years to accomplish his task, during which he passed the door of his own house thrice, and never had time to enter. Shun was so pleased with the skill and devotion of his agent that he appointed him his successor on the throne instead of his own unworthy son, and the nation had no reason to

UNDER- AND OVER-SHOT WHEELS.
(*By permission of Messrs. Newton and Co.*)

regret the choice. He surveyed all the country to the north of the Yang-tsze-Kiang, and divided it into nine provinces, which formed the first Empire of China, founded in the year 2,100 B.C. Yu is justly held up to the youth of the present time as the model of devotion and industry. He is said never to have lost 'an inch of time,' and during one meal he rose three times to give instructions to his Ministers.

It is characteristic of the high moral tone of these old rulers that Yu, who was the son of a man who had been executed for treason, instead of being put to death, as he would have been in the present day, was appointed to his father's post of engineer, and made ruler of the empire. Yao had passed a law that children were not to be put to death for the sins of their parents two or three hundred years before Moses published that law for the Jews. *A Mosaic law anticipated.*

For the next 439 years after Yu, the *Hea* dynasty ruled in China, from 2,205 to 1766 B.C. This was succeeded by the *Shang* dynasty, from 1766 to 1122 B.C., and that by the *Chow*, which lasted from 1122 to 255 B.C.—only three dynasties in 1850 years, implying a large measure of peace and prosperity in a country in which the *right* to depose a ruler who failed to satisfy the people was an acknowledged rule and custom. The change of dynasty was in no case a revolution. It was only an attempt to return to the ideal of all good government—that of Yao and Shun. *The Hea and Shang dynasties.*

Its illustrious men.

The last of these dynasties, though it dwindled away in weakness and dishonour, was made illustrious by a revival of learning, and the labours of the greatest men that China has ever produced. These were Confucius, Laotsze and Mencius. The two first flourished in the sixth, and Mencius in the fourth, century before Christ. These men exerted an influence greater far than that of any of the rulers of these long dynasties. Their pens were more powerful than sceptres, and Confucius has been called the 'uncrowned King' of China.

China's one revolutionary dynasty.

Chao, King of Chin, having overthrown the Chows, his son Chi established the fifth dynasty in 255 B.C., which he called after his own nation, the *Chin*, the name by which the country is known in the West as China. Chin, who called himself 'First Emperor,' by his military genius and autocratic despotism, crushed the liberties of the small States which had hitherto maintained their home rule while dependencies of the empire, conquered the nationalities south of the Yang-tsze-Kiang, and divided the empire into thirty-six provinces, appointing Governors of his own over them, and centralizing all authority in the capital, under his own control. This was the first, and we may say the only, *revolution* that has ever taken place in China. The number of provinces has been reduced to eighteen, but the system of government remains substantially the same as it was under Chi, but more constitutional, through the increased power of Government boards. After he had established his authority over the united empire, he set himself to secure himself against attack from without by building the Great Wall to protect his empire from the incursions of the wild Mongol and Manchu tribes on the north. This great undertaking he accomplished in ten years by employing the forced labour of a million of men—the only great work in China carried on by the oppression of the people—and his name has been held in execration in the country ever since.

The literati and the sacred literature of Chin being all opposed to his revolutionary methods, he ordered the sacred books compiled by Confucius to be given to the flames, and 460 of the most learned men of China were burned to death, lest the books should be restored from their retentive memories. It was during this dynasty that Taoism in its corrupt and superstitious form rose to power, its followers being favoured by the dynasty. *Slaughter of literati.*

The *Han* dynasty, which succeeded in establishing itself by the overthrow of the *Chin* in 206 B.C., is that of which Chinamen are most proud, and to this day they designate themselves as the men of Han. It was distinguished by general prosperity and by the revival of literature, favoured by the internal peace secured through the union of the empire so rudely established by the despotism of Chi, and protected from external assault by the *The Han dynasty.*

Great Wall which he had built. Taoism and Buddhism, which had both been patronized under the Chin dynasty, were discouraged, and Confucianism, which had been long under a cloud, was again restored to favour, and became more predominant and influential than ever.

It is not needful for our purpose to name each dynasty that sprang up, one after another, all alike based on the principle of *reformation* on the line of a return to the ideal of perfection shown in the days of Yao and Shun.

Discovery of the art of printing. The Tang dynasty, which flourished from 618 to 905 A.D., was illustrious for the number and excellence of its poets. The Hanlin Yuan, or Imperial Academy, the highest summit of literary ambition, was established, and the art of printing was discovered in the eighth century—500 years before it was said to have been discovered by Gutenberg. It is scarcely credible that the knowledge of Chinese block-printing was unknown in Europe long before Gutenberg's time; and the advance from the *block* to the *movable type* was a simple, we may say a necessary one, when the change was made from the Chinese symbolic characters to the letters of the Roman alphabet. Movable types had been made in China at a very early period, but have never superseded the printing from blocks to this day, except where missionaries have introduced the movable type. It was under this dynasty that pottery reached its highest perfection, and specimens of the ceramic art of the Han period are now bought at fabulous prices in European and Chinese markets.

The *Sung* dynasty, which ruled from 960 to 1180 A.D., was made famous by the rise of a school of philosophy noted for its metaphysical speculation and literary criticism. Under the guidance of its very able and learned leader, Chu-fu-tsze, it took an agnostic form, and by mythical theories worthy of a Strauss he did his best to get rid of every reference to Deity in the sacred books, and by sceptical speculation worthy of a Hume he tried to get rid of all that was supernatural. The Confucian school of thought was for a long time at a discount, and the school of Chu-fu-tsze triumphant, but in the long-run Chinese common-sense and honest investigation got the better of the negative philosophy and the higher criticism, and the orthodox school regained the ascendancy which it continues to hold over the Chinese mind. *Rise of philosophy and criticism.*

The *Yuen* dynasty marked a new era in the changes of government in China. It was begun in 1260, after a severe struggle, by the eruption of the Mongolian hordes, who, under their great leader Kublai Khan, carried his conquests over a greater portion of the northern hemisphere than any conqueror of ancient or modern times. The dynasty he founded maintained its sway from 1280 to 1368. Though Kublai subdued the country, he never changed the form of government. The higher intelligence and civilization of *The first foreign dynasty.*

the Chinese conquered the rude children of the wilds of the Arctic region. With a wise discretion they left the people in the full possession of their laws and religion. To him China owes her only monumental work besides the Great Wall —the Grand Canal from Peking to Hang-chau, a distance of 700 miles, connecting it with the old canal from Canton, making an inland waterway from the extreme north to the south of China, open at all seasons, and to all the intermediate towns, an immense boon at a time when the passage by sea could only be carried on at long intervals with the half-yearly change of the monsoons.

The Grand Canal.

After being subjected to a foreign yoke for almost a century, the native Ming dynasty established itself in 1368, and justified its designation of the *Bright* dynasty by its cultivation of literature in all departments, which it embodied in the systematic form of encyclopædias of vast dimensions, such as no other people have ever attempted, compared with which the 'Encyclopædia Britannica' is a small affair, though it includes a large field of science unknown to China. The codification of the laws of China was begun during this dynasty, though completed under the succeeding one, a work of great talent and utility, the criminal code being brought within such moderate compass as to be sold for a few pence, and expressed in language so simple that anyone can understand it.

The Ming dynasty.

During the later decadent period of the Mings, the insignificant and rude tribe of the Mongolian race—the Manchus—had crept down from their ice-bound home to the comparatively warmer climate to the north of the Great Wall. They were called in by a treacherous Chinese General, professedly to assist in putting down an insurrectionary movement, but in reality to assist his own ambitious schemes. They took advantage of their opportunity, and in a few years conquered the whole country for themselves, and established what they called the *Tsing* or Pure dynasty in 1644, which still holds its sway, but with a feeble grasp, through the support of European Powers, with doubtful advantage to the people, by whom it is detested. It would have been overthrown by the *Tai-ping* rebellion but for the interference of Englishmen—an interference alike unjustifiable and injurious.

Second foreign dynasty.

The earlier monarchs of this Manchu race showed their wisdom by adopting the same policy as that of Kublai Khan: they conformed their rude manners and customs to those of the Chinese, encouraged the literature of the country, and maintained the old laws and the ancestral religion. It has produced great rulers, both male and female. Of the latter the present Empress-Dowager is an illustrious example, and Kang-hi, who reigned from 1662 to 1723, will compare favourably with the best rulers of any age.

Causes of deterioration in the nineteenth century. During this century the government and people of China have deteriorated, chiefly through the encroachments and *excesses* of Western nations, partly from their own adhesion to ancient institutions and habits totally unsuited for the progressive development of the higher civilization of the human race. That Western, and we grieve to add *Christian*, nations have been guilty of much rudeness and injustice in their intercourse with China cannot be doubted. They used the tremendous forces with which science had armed them to break in upon a people whose government was framed only for the preservation of internal peace, not for aggressive wars, nor even for the defence of the country from foreign enemies, of whom there were none known to them against whom Nature had not provided a sufficient defence.

Responsibilities of civilization. Civilized nations may perhaps be justified in using force to control the lawless and cruel acts of savage races, but when they force themselves and their wars on a people with an organized government, just laws, and a civilization much more ancient than their own, it is sure to lead to disorganization, if not destruction. When to an unjustifiable employment of force you add the immoral practices of many of the representatives of our modern civilization, the frauds of trade, and the unholy traffic in pernicious and poisonous drugs, the evil is increased tenfold. The present impotence and degradation of China is in a great measure due to European

The History of the Chinese 79

wars and the opium trade, for which England is so largely responsible. They have lowered the prestige of the Government, and driven it to greater corruption in raising money, besides inflicting great evils upon the people.

While we deplore the evils inflicted by the corruptions which cling to the best of human institutions, and have no desire to minimize or excuse them, we must recognise the benefits which Western civilization has conferred on China, while we trust that many of the evils may prove temporary, and others were such as are inevitable in the breaking-up of the old order by the introduction of the new. China had reached a state of stagnation after centuries of progress, and stagnation is the precursor of decay and death. There was a necessity for some external movement to stir the stagnant pools of her political and social institutions; the old internal forces were exhausted or dead. This could not take place without disturbance and temporary disorder. The letting in of the purest light on decaying matter only hastens death, while it prepares the way for a new development of life and beauty. *[Compensating advantages.]*

It is admitted, even by the Chinese, that the wars of the English were carried on with the greatest possible regard for the lives and property of the civil population, and even of conquered enemies—a bright contrast to Chinese warfare. While there have been traders and trades which *[Favourable influences.]*

were a disgrace to Christian civilization, the Chinese fully admit the high regard for truth and honour, and for sympathy and generosity, in the great body of our merchants, while they cannot for a moment question the character of our Government officials for integrity and justice, and the lives of missionaries for purity and beneficence. These influences have told on the public mind, though our presence is still offensive, and our interference resented.

Christianity is slowly but surely telling on the people, not merely by the conversion of individuals, but far more widely by the awaking of thought and the enlarging of the mind by the introduction of new ideas. Educational missions are raising up a race of men who are already taking their place as a new force in Chinese life, and the higher classes at the seat of Government are availing themselves of the mission colleges for the acquisition of the English language and Western science; even the Emperor has studied English under men trained in a college founded by the Chinese Government, of which an American missionary is the president.

In estimating the forces at work for the enlightenment and elevation of China, we by no means limit them to those of Christian missions, all-important as these are; commerce, and many of our commercial men, play an important part. Applied science, with its steamers and railroads and telegraphs, is a beneficent revolutionary power. The large staff of our Government servants in the ambassadorial and consular service, many of them men of high character and ability, have done much to prepare the way for the regeneration of China. One of them, who was transferred to the Chinese Government—Sir Robert Hart—has done more than any living man for the promotion of truth and righteousness in China. Even our wars, bad as they were, have shown the Chinese how to temper conquest with clemency, and to exercise power with moderation and justice.

With all these influences at work on a people possessed of the mental and moral qualities displayed during an unbroken history of 4,000 or 5,000 years, there is good reason to hope that China will one day be in the future what she has been in the past, the greatest power in the eastern hemisphere of the world. *Hope for the future.*

GOVERNMENT.

The government of China is a patriarchal autocracy, both civil and religious, a vain attempt to carry out in a great empire what Providence only meant to apply to a family or clan. Even from the days of Abraham God anticipated the establishment of a kingly form of government. The promise to the patriarch, in Genesis xvii., was not only that he would be the father of a numerous offspring, but that he *Patriarchal government.*

would be the father of a race of kings : ' Kings shall come out of thee.' The combination of the ruling power and priestly office was broken up on the departure from Egypt, by the establishment of the priesthood in the tribe of Levi, and the arrangement for a future race of kings of the tribe of Judah, as Jacob, before his death, had foretold in his prophetic blessing of his sons, and which Moses provided for, by the Divine command, by laying down rules for the future election and regulation to the kingly power.

<small>Limitations on autocracy.</small> Though the government of China is patriarchal and nominally autocratic, it is limited by important and beneficial restraints which make it in some degree *constitutional*. The following checks on *absolute* government may be named :

First of all, the Emperor is practically bound to rule according to the example and precepts of the early founders of the empire, especially those of Yao and Shun. These are, to the rulers of China, what the example and precepts of Moses were to the ruler of the Jews. The King was ordered to write a copy of the laws of God with his own hand.

Second, the throne is held on the understanding that the Emperor rules as Heaven's representative for the good of the people. This is explicitly expressed in the sacred books, in which he is called ' Heaven's officer,' and is told that ' The real way to serve Heaven is to love the people,' and that ' if he fails to love the people

Heaven will for the sake of the people cast him out.' These truths are acknowledged by the Emperor in prayers which he offers publicly every year at the 'altar of heaven.'

Third, the right of the people to rebel and dethrone any oppressive ruler is distinctly understood alike by the Emperor and the people. It is laid down in their sacred books, which are held in highest honour by all, and Confucius quotes the example of two of the greatest of the early Emperors of China, who founded dynasties on the dethronement of their predecessors. Ching Tung is celebrated in the Shoo-King for having overthrown the Hea dynasty, 1766 B.C., because Heaven had decreed the destruction of its last ruler on account of his despotism, and Woo Wang, in 1112 B.C., is equally praised for carrying out the decree of Heaven for the overthrow of the last Emperor of the Shang dynasty, because he oppressed the people.

Fourth, the government is carried on by a Cabinet and Council which, though chosen by the Emperor, are held in such high esteem by the people that none but a very strong ruler could override their decision. Besides, there are certain men of the highest character who are appointed as censors, who boldly protest against any material departure from the constitutional laws or usage of former times. These men have often been faithful to the death in opposing the will of despotic Emperors.

Last of all, the power of the Emperor is checked by the limitation of his army. The only troops directly under his control are the Manchus, who are not only limited in number, but scattered throughout the vast territory, with no power of concentration or united action. All the Chinese troops are under the control of the Civil Governor of each province, and are more like a militia or an armed police force for the preservation of peace, than a regular army. This is a more effective check on despotic power than even the English control of the ' sinews of war ' by keeping hold of the purse-strings in the House of Commons.

There is one thing which shows that the government of China is largely dependent on the good-will of the people : that is, the regular circulation of what is generally called the *Pekin Gazette*—the oldest newspaper in the world, if we may call it by so modern a name. It is issued by the Government, and contains an account of all the proceedings of the Emperor and his Cabinet and Council, and of the six Boards established for the different departments of the State. It is sent to all parts of the empire for the information of the officials, and is published for the use of all, and often republished in different places for free circulation or sale. This publicity implies a necessity for ruling in a way that secures the approval and good-will of the people.

Administration.

A corrupt executive. The administration of the government is allowed by experts to be excellent *in theory*, and would be good in practice, if only it were honestly carried out. But, alas! the practice is corrupt to the core. With a few honourable exceptions, from the Governors of provinces to the lowest police runners of the inferior courts of justice, the officials are influenced by bribes, which are forcibly exacted if not freely offered. The laws are good, and taxes light, but the exactions of officers and collectors are a burden and curse to the country.

The criminal code. The criminal code of China now lying before us is a model of justice, simplicity, and common-sense. Almost the only thing one objects to is the too liberal use of the bamboo as the means of punishment, but the Chinese prefer it to imprisonment. Compared with the Gentoo code of the Hindus, it is as light to darkness. Sir George Stanton, who translated it, says: 'The criminal code of China will bear comparison with the laws of Rome or of modern Europe.' One feature in its composition is worthy of note. It is written in a style so clear and simple that it can be understood by the humblest of the people, if they can read at all, and can be bought for a few pence, so that everyone may know the law and the punishment due for its violation.

All equal in the eye of the law.
Before this law all are placed in a position of almost perfect equality—not as in the native laws of India, where the Brahman, the Sudra, and the Paria is treated each according to a different rule. Till lately even the laws of the States of Europe made a great difference between the freeman and the serf. There is in China a form of mild domestic slavery, but the law is substantially the same for slave and free man. For the murder of a free man the sentence is death by *decapitation*. For the murder of a slave a free man has the privilege of *being hanged*. This may seem a doubtful privilege to European or American tastes, but it is highly prized by Chinamen, who have a great objection to being 'sent to their ancestors' with their heads off; they consider it disrespectful to their parents, who brought them into the world with their heads properly fixed on their shoulders.

Bonds of unity.
When we take into account the duration of this great empire, ruling over a fourth part of the population of the world, and for a period of 4,000 years, we must admit that there is something in the race of men of which it is composed, or the institutions which they have established, which marks them out as exceptional and superior in respect of some important qualities which demand our esteem and study.

It is not by the external conditions of either physical forces or the boundaries or features of the country that China has preserved its unity so

Administration

long. There are broad rivers and high mountain chains which seem to suggest and encourage the division of the empire into several large kingdoms, as there were in early times. It is not by the triumph of matter over mind, but by the triumph of mind over matter, that China has been maintained in its unity. Its government, its laws, and its language have bound the people together in moral fetters which outward and adverse forces could not sunder.

Japanese triumph. It is, however, difficult to recognise superiority in a race which has of late allowed itself to be out-matched and conquered by a small and hitherto insignificant country like Japan. But this sad fact is easily accounted for on grounds which reflect little discredit on the courage or patriotism of the Chinese, while they bring out features in the old maxims of government which command the respect of the lovers of peace and benevolence.

Government by moral force. It has always been a fundamental principle in China that the government of the country *must not be by force, but by the willing subjection of the people to a beneficent ruler*, and when the Emperor could not by good government secure the affections and confidence of the people, he was unfit to rule, and the people had a constitutional right to depose him. The Shoo-King, the most ancient and sacred of the Chinese classics—a book which is committed to memory by every scholar in China, including every ruler and official, from the

Emperor to the lowest magistrate—contains the following words:

'Heaven establishes Sovereigns merely for the sake of the people; whom the people desire for Sovereign, him will Heaven protect; whom the people dislike as Sovereign, him will Heaven reject.'

It was a fundamental principle from the earliest times *that the nation was to be governed by moral power rather than by physical force*. For this reason the army in China has always been small, and only sufficient for the preservation of order and the defence of the country, the chief dependence being on a militia. War has not been lauded, and soldiers have not been held in honour, as in other countries.

Civil power predominates. Although the present Manchu dynasty was founded by conquest, and warriors became masters of the country, the old law of China was respected, either from necessity or policy. The *civil* power was made *predominant*, and the highest *military* honours were made *subordinate* to those of the *civil* service—an arrangement unknown among the Christian Powers of Europe—the theory being that by getting the ablest and best men to rule and administer the affairs of the country, the people would always be willing to obey their rulers and live in peace. For this the sages wrought out their system of education and selection of officials of all kinds by examinations. This optimistic confidence in the pure love of virtue has frequently been rudely shaken. This might be shown by the treatment which Confucius met with at the hands of his countrymen in his lifetime, and by the history of the empire.

But the end is not yet. The difficulties of Japan are yet to come, and are not far off. China has great recuperative force still latent in the

<small>There still is hope.</small>

A MANDARIN REVIEWING ARCHERS.
(*By permission of Messrs. Newton and Co.*)

undeveloped resources of the country and in the character of her phlegmatic population, slow of movement in the individual, and much slower in the mass of so large a country and so vast a population, but, when moved, susceptible of great progress and possessed of vast resources and tremendous force.

We anticipate a renewal of vital power in

China, not merely because the empire is ancient, and has maintained its unity and independence for so long a time; but from the character of the people who framed the constitution and upheld the laws with such conservative tenacity, and have so often recovered from great disasters, and regained order and prosperity, after years of anarchy and disorder which would have broken in pieces much more compact and manageable nations. If let alone, China would, ere long, 'right herself,' like a well-built lifeboat that has been submerged by a wave. There is both buoyancy and ballast in the Chinese mind and character.

Causes of Disaster.

The following, among others, are the causes which have of late led to disaster and the threatening of ruin :

1. The upholding of a foreign despotism alien to the interests and feelings of the people, who do not care to fight for their oppressors. This foreign Manchu dynasty has been upheld directly or indirectly by European Powers, when Chinamen would have driven them from the throne by their *constitutional right* of rebellion.

2. The Manchus have violated the sacred right of election to offices through fair competition by selling offices and titles to raise revenue. By this perversion of one of the most cherished customs of the country the Emperor has brought into places of trust and power a lower and greedier class of men, who feel they have purchased a right to plunder the people.

3. The army, small in comparison with the extent of country and population, has been reduced and demoralized by officers not receiving their pay, and being driven to the expedient of sending home their men to earn a living, while they drew payment for them as if they were in the ranks. The subjection of the soldiers in each province to the authority of the Provincial Governor divides the army into many independent sections, and delays if it does not prevent concentration.

4. By the neglect of modern implements of warfare, as used by Western nations; who have made war a perfect science of destruction. China has neglected this from her old habit of treating all outside nations with contempt, which she could well do until Christian nations from the West came with their new implements of war, and taught her old neighbour and former dependency, Japan, to imitate their example.

5. That China has not adopted Western fashions, like Japan, is not surprising if we take into account that not only was China a peaceable nation from inclination and interest, but averse from ancient custom to make *force* the basis of governing. Even foreign countries, according to the theory of Confucius, were to be subdued by *the example* of good government at home—a theory which has been rudely exploded by the invention of gunpowder and foreign invasion. It is easy to understand how the Japanese should imitate foreign customs. They have been an imitative race all along. All their literature, manufactures and arts were borrowed from China. China, on the other hand, originated her own civilization without borrowing from any, and it is not easy for an old and great nation to change its time-honoured customs.

6. Japan, a small country and mercurial people, could easily adopt the new arts of destruction, and by quietly preparing while China slept in fancied security, it was easy to gain temporary advantages over the unprepared giant just awakened out of his long sleep. But for fear of European interference China exhausted the resources of Japan by passive resistance until prepared for action.

7. The exhaustion of Chinese resources, ruin of her prestige by the repeated wars and exactions of European Powers, and the injury inflicted on her people by the spread of the opium habit, for which England is so largely responsible, crippled her efforts and disheartened the defenders in a war for which they were in every way so ill prepared.

CHAPTER V.

EDUCATION AND LITERATURE.

National education. THE encouragement of education has always been considered the glory of China, and rightly so, although the extent to which it is carried on has been much exaggerated. The ideal of the Emperors of China was to have an elementary school in every village, elementary and high schools in each town, schools and a college in the cities, with a system of competitive examinations for all Government posts in the capital, so the ablest men might be secured for the government and administration of the country. But while the examinations have been kept up, the ideal of a national system of education for all the people has not been realized. Government, like the University of London, is an examining, not a teaching, body. It has encouraged the higher education of the few by dispensing the honours and employments of the State only to scholars, and that by an elaborate system of examinations, so that the poorest can rise to the highest rank and greatest power under the Emperor. China is the only country in the world in which the titles of honour for the peaceful pursuit of learning are higher and more lucrative than those conferred on warriors or priests. The most successful General takes a lower place than a scholar who bears a degree of Han Lin, similar to that of our LL.D. or D.C.L.

Highest reward in the 'Civil' Service.

There are four degrees conferred on scholars. They cannot be accurately compared with those given in Europe, but roughly they may be classed thus: *Siu tsai*, or 'budding scholar,' which is generally said to correspond to our B.A., but is much more like the matriculation of a youth who has passed his first examination, as the title seems to imply. Even this degree confers on its owner much distinction in his village, and confers a title on his father equivalent to that of 'father of a *siu tsai*.' It also exempts the bearer of the title from being sentenced to be beaten by the magistrate, no mean privilege in a country where all kinds of faults are punished by strokes of the bamboo. The examination takes place in provincial towns all over the country. The second is held in the capital of each of the eighteen provinces on the same days, and those who pass are called *ku jin*, or 'promoted men,' corresponding to our B.A. degree. The third title, *tsin sz*, or 'entered scholar,' is conferred by examination in the capital, and resembles our degree of M.A. The final examination entitles the successful candidate to the coveted distinction of *Han Lin* and mem-

Examinations for office.

bership of the Imperial Academy, with a certain allowance until he obtains an official appointment.

Talent only encouraged. This kind of encouragement of learning has no tendency to promote general education; it rather tends to discourage it. It is only the more promising students who have any chance of rising high enough to profit much by study, and the poor are tempted to spend all their money in the education of one member of the family or village clan in hope of his being able to confer both honours and fortune on those who have assisted him to rise. It reminds one of the ambition of Scotch families of the humbler order to have one son educated for the Church, but from much purer motives. They have not the Chinaman's hope of riches for either the son or themselves; their sole reward is that of advancing their boy to the useful but poorly-paid post of minister, with the privilege of seeing him ' wag his pow in a pupit '; and while the one child was sent to college, the rest of the family were not denied the advantage of the school.

Doubtful results. The theory of the Chinese Government is good, in so far as it aims at getting the ablest men of the country for the posts of legislation and administration, but, like many good theories, it sadly fails in the practical results. The best men are not necessarily those who pass the highest in a written examination, and this kind of education and examination is not likely to produce the highest development of the intellect, and the best moral qualities for high office. The education is a laborious system of cramming with obsolete and useless learning, entirely based on the one set of ancient books handed down by Confucius. The man who is surest to get a degree is the man who has committed the four sacred books and the five classics to memory, and can most readily quote them in his essays. He is sure to succeed if he learns and quotes Yao and Shun, who were the best of rulers 4,000 years ago, but not up to the requirements of the nineteenth century. But that the system has been, on the whole, beneficial cannot be doubted, especially if compared with the common practice in the East, where unworthy favourites are often put in places of highest trust, and rulers surround themselves with ignorant parasites, who too often rise to power by encouraging the vices of their masters. A Chinese Emperor could never make a eunuch or a favourite page or barber his Prime Minister, or even a member of his Council.

LETTERS AND LANGUAGE.

The form of Chinese letters, now so complex and arbitrary, seems to have been originally representative of natural objects, as will be seen from the following specimen taken from Dr. Morrison's 'Miscellany.' The symbols are said to have been invented by Tseng-hi 2,800 years before Christ: *Origin of letters.*

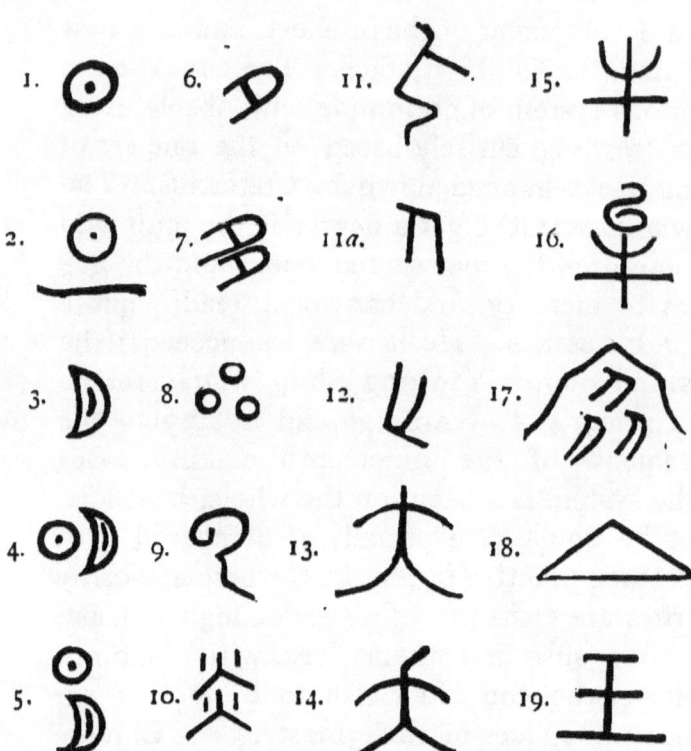

1. The sun. 2. The sun rising—the morning. 3. The moon. 4. The light of sun and moon united; hence, morning, splendid, bright. 5. Sun and moon rising and setting, meaning to alternate; alternation, exchange. 6. The moon half seen, or evening. 7. Two evenings, or frequent occurrence; often, many. 8. Stars. 9. Clouds. 10. The symbol for flame repeated; a blaze, luminous, glorious. 11 and 11*a*. A human being. 12. Human being upside down; to change the state of, to transform, to convert. 13. Man with his arms and legs spread out; hence, large, great. 14. Man with head hanging on one side; mummy, weak, delicate. 15. Symbol for horned cattle of all kinds. 16. The breath issuing from the mouth of a cow; hence, to blow, to bellow, to advance, to encroach. 17. A house with three human beings within it, or a family. 18. Three united in one, or a triad. 19. One uniting three; he who rules others, a king. This etymology is attributed to Confucius, kings being in his eyes a bond of union.

Education and Literature

The form of these symbols soon got changed to suit the convenience of writers; and to enlarge their vocabulary it was needful to increase the number of symbols, which could not be copied from Nature, and became altogether arbitrary, and more and more complex. Some requiring as many as seventeen strokes of the pencil to form one radical or root of a word, the word itself might have a great many more. Letters, in the proper sense of the word, they have none. The 214 radicals, varying from one stroke to seventeen, are the nearest approach to our letters of the alphabet. But even these give no intelligible clue to either the sound or meaning of the character of which they form a part, with possibly between twenty and thirty strokes of the pen, or rather pencil, of fine hair with which it was formed. *[Complex and inconvenient.]*

This complexity, or rather perplexity, in the Chinese character is the great obstacle to the general education of the people of China, and the only hope for the many is the introduction of an alphabetic form of printing and writing. Christians are getting more and more into the way of using the Roman letters, and find it a great boon. The children of Christian parents learn to read and write by this system in about a tenth part of the time it takes the heathen child to master the difficulties of the Chinese characters. The old and widespread idea that China was a nation of 400,000,000 of readers has been rudely dispelled. Not only must we deduct little children and *[Hinders education.]*

women from this number, but even of the men it is computed that not one in twenty can read intelligently. Even this gives a wide opening to Christian literature, and one reader in a village is proud to exercise his gifts for the benefit of all. The great obstacle to the introduction of any new system lies in the pride of educated Chinamen; they love their own language, and are proud of the beauty of its characters, which convey the ideas through the eye to the mind with the directness of a picture, independent of the aid of sound by the circuitous route of the ear, as in other languages, which generally require both the ear and the eye to complete the intelligent perception of the meaning.

The tone in Chinese. The written or printed character has the great advantage of being understood by all scholars over the length and breadth of China, with its many millions; but if read aloud it needs to be rendered in the vernacular of a great number of districts, which cannot understand each other's spoken language, though the scholars in all of them could understand the same book by looking on the page. Not only must they give the spoken words of each district, but the *tone* of each word, high or low, rising, falling, or circumflex. The neglect of these tones, even when the words are otherwise correctly sounded, may cause the greatest mistakes, giving a meaning the very opposite of what was intended, or a sense so ridiculous that the listeners to the gravest dis-

Education and Literature

course cannot help bursting into fits of laughter. For example, the word *chu* in one tone means *a lord*, in another tone it means *a pig*, so that a stranger may be, as he thinks, speaking of a noble lord, but by using the wrong tone he may call him a noble pig. In recent caricatures which excited persecution, a pig, by this play upon the tone, was profanely pictured as the object of Christian worship. The word *tung* in one tone means *soup*, and in another tone it means *sugar*. An honoured missionary of our acquaintance, who was careless of his tone, told his cook, as he thought, to buy a fowl and make soup; but, using the wrong tone, he really told him to buy a fowl and make sugar. The simple or waggish cook went and asked another missionary if they had a way of making sugar out of fowls in America.

There are said to be a hundred vernacular languages or local dialects in China, in which the natives of one district cannot understand the spoken language of the others, besides many more in which the differences are not so great as to be quite unintelligible.

The change of the written character into the spoken language is also perplexing, and far from easy even to the natives. It may be illustrated by the first four words in the first verse of John's Gospel in the Amoy vernacular, taking the Roman letters for both. _{Written and spoken language.}

The *written* characters would be, GOAN SI EU TO (In the beginning was the Word). The spoken language would be, 'Khi thau u To li.' Both would have the same meaning. The former would only be understood by a scholar; the second would be understood by all. Many who acquire sufficient instruction to enable them to carry on business and keep accounts never learn enough to read a book, far less to understand it. As for the women of China, not one in tens of thousands is ever taught the simplest elements of their language. It is computed that there are not more than 12,000,000 or 15,000,000 of its 400,000,000 who can read so as to understand an ordinary work. In one generation the British Government has raised up in India a larger number of readers than China can boast of after thousands of years of civilization. One great evil resulting from this difficulty in acquiring the language is, that the man who does become a scholar is regarded as a prodigy, and acquires an influence far beyond his moral and intellectual merits. The literati are the despots of China, and are the chief sources of opposition to new, and above all foreign, improvements, which would be fatal to their ascendancy and even to their livelihood.

The system of education. The difficulty of acquiring a knowledge of the written character is not the worst obstacle in the way of becoming an intelligent reader of the Chinese language. The system of education is the great hindrance to education in the proper sense of the term. The pupil is required to go on learning the form of the characters for years

Education and Literature

without getting the slightest idea of their meaning—a most discouraging and stupefying process. It does strengthen the memory, but it is by the sacrifice of the intellectual powers, which are not developed even at the later stages of study. There is no attempt at *drawing out* the faculties of the mind, which is not only the etymological, but the rational, definition of the great object of education. The strengthening of memory is good, but in China it is purchased at too great a price. These difficulties result in the great mass of the people being uneducated.

CHINESE LITERATURE.

The ancient literature of China is its chief glory; not that it can vie with the literary productions of Greece and Rome in their incomparable beauties of imagination and language, or with the writings of Moses for lofty conceptions of God and authoritative revelations of Divine truth, but for antiquity of written documents it excels that of all lands. Literature recently discovered in Egyptian tombs, and in Babylonian libraries dug up from the bowels of the earth, may be a little older, but that of China has continued to this day the living language of a great empire.

The sacred books of the Chinese have been a moral power in the formation of the character of the people such as no books except those of the

The sacred books.

Hebrew and Christian Scriptures have ever been, while in the purity of thought and morality of their teaching no heathen books can be for a moment compared with them. Dr. James Legge, the highest authority on the character of the sacred books of China, which he has translated from the first to the last, told the writer that *there was not an expression in any of these books which he would be ashamed to read aloud in the presence of his daughters*—the strongest expression which a stanch old Puritan could use.

Genuine and authentic. The genuineness and authenticity of these old records of the past, as collected by Confucius in the sixth century before Christ, are now placed beyond doubt. They have undergone the severest scrutiny from critics of all kinds, much the same as that to which our own Scriptures have been subjected, including that of the *higher criticism*. They have had their enemies. They were at one time almost entirely destroyed by the Emperor Chi, 200 years before Christ; every copy that could be found was burned, and the learned men who had committed them to memory were all destroyed, that the imperishable record of them in their hearts might be buried in their graves. After the death of this despot every effort was made to restore them, and one blind old scholar, who, from his obscurity, had escaped persecution, was able to repeat the whole from memory, to scribes appointed for the purpose, with wonderful fidelity. At a later time, on

Education and Literature

pulling down an old house, a complete copy was found, and compared with that taken down from the lips of the scholar. These resembled what we now call *recensions* of the Scriptures, and were the foundation of two schools of critics, until the common-sense of Chinese scholarship led to a compromise on the small discrepancies in the two sets of manuscripts.

Long before the sceptical age and schools of higher criticism arose on the Continent of Europe, there arose an agnostic school in China, during the twelfth century of the Christian era, which subjected the *sacred books* to a criticism very much like that to which the Bible has recently been subjected. They eliminated the idea of a personal Deity, and turned into myths or legends many parts of the venerable old books. But here again the common-sense of the Chinaman has got rid of that *negative* criticism, from which, in this century, Biblical scholars have not yet emancipated themselves, though we doubt not they eventually will, and we shall have our old Bible proved to be as genuine, authentic, and credible a record as the sacred books of China now are in the eyes of the masses of the people, both learned and unlearned. *The agnostic school.*

The records which Confucius handed down with so much care date their origin from more than 2,200 years before Christ, the date generally fixed on for the earliest authentic specimens of Egyptian literature and Babylonian translations from Accadian documents. A striking and suggestive coincidence.

THE SACRED CLASSICS.

<small>The four books and five classics.</small> We cannot give an analysis of the *four books* and *five classics* which constitute the sacred literature of China—it would occupy too much of our space. We may say it is not sacred in the sense of being chiefly taken up with religious or heavenly themes. They do contain references to sacred subjects, and are neither agnostic nor sceptical; but the views of Confucius about the *invisible* and *eternal* were vague and uncertain, and he felt that he had no mission to teach men about what he did not himself know definitely or certainly. He faithfully recorded what the ancients believed on these matters, of which he felt the importance, and writes with reverence, as we shall show when we treat of the religions of China; but he felt that his mission was to teach the people how to live in this world, and to teach their kings and statesmen how to rule, so as to promote peace, righteousness, and prosperity by imitating the ancient rulers of the country.

<small>Their great influence.</small> Confucius fulfilled his mission with fearless fidelity and unflagging zeal, and, with the exceptions of Moses and the Apostle Paul, no man has exerted so deep and lasting an influence on so large a portion of the human race. That the

influence has been on the whole beneficial to China, the unparalleled duration of so large an empire, and the general prosperity and welfare of the people, are the best proof. The Empires of Babylon and Egypt, which started in the race of civilization about the same time with that of China, perished before half the period of Chinese history had run its course. The Greek and Roman Empires, which began to flourish a thousand or fifteen hundred years later, have disappeared, while China remains the largest empire in the world under her old laws and primitive constitution.

That the Chinese are right in attributing their duration and prosperity to Confucius as a collator and expounder of the ancient classics of China there can be no doubt. They have a common saying, 'There is no one like Confucius; before Confucius there never was a Confucius; since Confucius there has never been a Confucius.' They have surrounded his memory with a halo of Divinity, and worship him with honours only inferior to that of the Supreme God. They give a description of the sage so exaggerated as to make him appear ridiculous in the eyes of foreigners, but impress one with the idea that he was a *thorough Chinaman*, a fact which to a large extent explains the secret of his influence on his countrymen. They go so far as to say that his face was a map of China. The following is the description of the sage, by no means flattering,

[margin: Influence of Confucius.]

taken by Dr. Morrison from the high authority, Kang-hi's dictionary:

Description of Confucius.

'His face showed in miniature the five mountains and the four great rivers. He had a high forehead, a protruding chin, two high cheek-bones, and high aquiline nose to represent the five mountains. His mouth stood open and showed his teeth. His nose was contorted so as to exhibit his nostrils. His eyes exhibited a protruding pupil, and his ears were so large as to attract notice, in this resembling the four great rivers. He was very tall, some say 9½ cubits in height, and his hands hung down below his knees. His eyebrows exhibited twelve shades of colour, and from his eyes beamed sixty-four intelligences. He stood like the Fung-bird perched, and he sat like Long-tsun the dragon couchant. The highest excellences of the greatest sages of China were found in Confucius. He had the forehead of Yao and the back of Tao, and so of all the virtues of previous monarchs and great men who had shone in Chinese history.'

Previous to the birth of the sage, the sacred Lin bird discharged from its stomach precious writing containing the following inscription: '*A son, the pure essence of water; a successor of the fallen fortunes of Chow; a plain-robed King; one who shall rule without ever ascending a throne.*' On the evening of his birth two dragons wound around the house, heavenly music sounded in the ear of his mother, and when he was born an inscription appeared on his breast with these words: 'The maker of a rule for settling the world.' Whatever we may say of these extravagant expressions, written long after the sage had died a poor and neglected man, they show the high estimation in which this favourite of the empire has been held for 2,000 years.

The great fault in the teaching of Confucius is its materialistic character and tendency. Its great defect is the absence of *definite* instruction about God and a future state, and the consequent want of the highest sanction for faith and motives for moral conduct. The aim of the sage was thoroughly good, his maxims are wise and pure; but more than wise sayings and pure teachings are required to check the tendency to evil, and to stimulate men to pure living. Defect of his teaching.

The following is a very brief account of the sacred books of the Chinese, commonly called the Four Books and the Five Classics.

The 'Book of Records,' or history, of which only fifty-eight out of a hundred sections have been preserved, is obscure from its great antiquity and incompleteness. It places the principles of good government in the heart, as illustrated in the lives of Yao and Shun, and their successors in the first dynasty, beginning 2356 B.C. The principles of government are four: Virtue, benevolence, gravity, sincerity. These virtues of the heart, they say, in their laconic style, 'Preserved, then order; lost, then anarchy.' Examples are The 'Shoo King,' or History.

given of these virtues in the Emperor Yao. The following is in an illustration of his teaching: '*Virtue, the people, territory, revenue,* is the order in which rulers are required to devote their attention to the order of Nature, which Heaven will approve, and Shang Ti (the Supreme Ruler) will regard with complacency. If this order be reversed, and *revenue* be made the first and *virtue* the last, then the people's hearts will be lost, Heaven's decree in favour of the existing ruler will be forfeited, Shang Ti's displeasure will be incurred, and the throne be given to another.'

The right of insurrection. Strange to say, in a book held in such high honour, not only by the people, but by the Emperors of every dynasty for more than 2,000 years, the *right of insurrection* against a bad ruler is openly declared as a law of Heaven. It is asserted that 'the people's hearts and Heaven's decree are the same,' the form of the Western saying, *Vox populi, vox Dei*. The oaths of the conspirators under the usurper Tang, who rose against and deposed the cruel tyrant Ki, are given, and the conspirator is highly praised. Wu Wang is also celebrated for rebelling against his former Sovereign, and both Tang and Wu were founders of dynasties.

The character of Yu. The following is a description of the Emperor Yu, who ascended the throne in 2200 B.C.: 'He condescended to his Ministers with easy grace; he ruled the country with generous forbearance; his punishments were limited to the criminals, and were not inflicted on their children, but his

Education and Literature

rewards were transmitted to future generations; he pardoned *inadvertent* faults, however great, but punished *deliberate* crime, however small. In cases of *doubtful crimes*, he dealt with them lightly, but of doubtful *merit* he showed the highest esteem. Rather than put to death the guiltless, he ran the risk of irregularity and laxity.' Such wise and beneficent rule cannot be paralleled in the history of any other country in that *early* period of the world's history.

The 'Shi King,' or 'Book of Odes,' is a collection of the best of the songs and poetry of different kinds illustrative of the life of the ancients. Confucius attached great importance to them, and urged kings and statesmen to study them, that they might know the habits and feelings of the people and rulers of olden times. He seems to have anticipated the familiar saying, 'Give me the making of the songs of a people, and I will leave others to make their laws.' Dr. Legge has not only made a translation in prose, but, with the assistance of friends, has turned them into poetic and most readable form. Some of the most interesting are rendered in good broad Scotch.

The book contains descriptions of political characters, both laudatory and satirical, veiled censure on eminent persons, many love-songs, the complaints of soldiers serving on distant frontiers, occasional delineations of nature, and the outpouring of the feelings on many subjects. None are immoral in their teaching, and, as Confucius

[sidenote: The 'Shi King,' or Book of Odes.]

said, for the right perusal of the 300 odes contained in the book it was needful to have 'thought not depraved,' the Chinese expression for 'purity of heart.' There were many vicious songs of the same period, but Confucius sternly excluded them all. Poetical merit, unaccompanied by moral worth, was of no value in his estimation.

Notions of poetry. The notions of the Chinese about poetry are thus given by Dr. Morrison:

'Human *feelings*, when excited in the breast, become embodied in *words*. When words fail to express them, sighs, or inarticulate tones of admiration and other sentiments, succeed. When these *sighs* and *aspirations* are inadequate to do justice to feeling, then recourse is had to *song*, and when the *song* or *hymn* is still found insufficient, man naturally expresses the intensity of his feelings by the action of his hands and the motion of his feet, or, as the Chinese language expresses it, he "hands it, gesticulates it, foots it, stamps it. . . . Poetry, more than anything else, moves heaven and earth, and agitates demons and gods.'

Specimens of poetry. We give a few verses as examples, all from Confucius' edition of the classics, 500 B.C. Some of them are 1,500 or 2,000 years before even that early date. We quote from the popular edition which Dr. Legge and his friends have turned into very literal verse.

The following is a covert allusion to King Wan's choice of the humblest to be his Ministers, if only virtuous and able — two of them were said to have been rabbit-catchers—written between 1184 and 1076 B.C.

> 'Carefully he sets his rabbit-nets all round :
> Chang-Chung his blows upon the pegs resound.
> Stalwart the man and bold! His bearing all
> Shows he might be his Prince's shield and wall.'

War comes in for celebration. Here is a description of an officer of Ch'ing about 800 B.C.:

> 1. 'How glossy is the lambkin's fur,
>   Smooth to the touch and fair to view!
>   In it arrayed, that officer
>   Rests in his lot to virtue true.
>
>   *   *   *   *   *
>
> 3. 'Splendid his robe of lambkin's fur,
>   With its three decorations grand :
>   It well becomes that officer,
>   The pride and glory of our land.'

Domestic ties are not infrequently referred to, and the mutual affection of husband and wife is often a subject of song. The following is a picture of the feelings of husbands on setting out on a desperate campaign :

> 1. 'List to the thunder and roll of the drum ;
>   See how we spring and brandish the dart !
>   Some raise Tsaou's walls, some do field work at home ;
>   But we to the southward lonely depart.
>
> 2. 'Our chief, Sun Tsze-Chung, agreement has made
>   Our forces to join with Chin and with Sung.
>   When shall we back from this service be led ?
>   Our hearts are all sad, and our courage unstrung.
>
>   *   *   *   *   *

4. 'For death as for life, at home or abroad,
    We pledged to our wives our faithfullest word;
   Their hands clasped in ours, together we vowed
    We'd live to old age in sweetest accord.

5. 'This march to the south can end but in ill.
    Oh! never again shall we our wives meet.
   The word that we pledged we cannot fulfil;
    Us home-returning they never will greet.'

Shi King, p. 82.

A SAMPLE OF A PROVINCIAL ARMY.
(*By permission of Messrs. Newton and Co.*)

'A WIFE DEPLORES HER HUSBAND'S ABSENCE.

1. 'Away the startled pheasant flies,
    With lazy movement of his wings.
   Borne was my husband from my eyes;
    What pain the separation brings!

2. 'The pheasant, though no more in view,
    His cry above, below, forth sends.
   Alas! my princely lord, 'tis you—
    Your absence—that my bosom rends.

Education and Literature

3. 'At sun and moon I sit and gaze,
   In converse with my troubled heart.
   Far, far from me my husband stays:
   When will he come to heal its smart?

4. 'Ye princely men who with him mate,
   Say, mark ye not his virtuous way?
   His rule is, Covet naught, none hate;
   How can his step from goodness stray?'

   Shi King, p. 83.

The evils of polygamy come out in the following wail over her husband's preference for his second wife:

1. 'Fierce is the wind and cold;
   And such is he.
   Smiling he looks, and, bold,
   Speaks mockingly.

   * * * *

2. 'As clouds of dust wind-blown,
   Just such is he.
   Ready he seems to own,
   And come to me.
   But he comes not nor goes,
   Stands in his pride;
   Long, long, with painful throes,
   Grieved I abide.

3. 'Strong blew the wind; the cloud
   Hastened away;
   Soon dark again, the shroud
   Covers the day.
   I wake, and sleep no more
   Visits my eyes;
   His course I, sad, deplore
   With heavy sighs.

   Ibid., p. 81.

'A LOYAL ODE TO A YOUNG PRINCE.

1. 'What trees grow on the Chung-nan hill?
   The white fir and the plum.
   In fur of fox, 'neath broidered robe,
   Thither our prince is come.
   His face glows with vermilion hue;
   Oh, may he prove a ruler true!

2. 'What find we on the Chung-nan hill?
    Deep nooks and open glade.
    Our prince shows there the double *ke*
    On lower robes displayed.
    His pendant holds each tinkling gem.
    Long life be his, and deathless fame !'
Shi King, p. 61.

A judicious lover finds the adored one engaged in home industry, but adorned with many accomplishments:

1. 'To steep your hemp you seek the moat,
    Where lies the pool the gate beyond ;
  I seek that lady good and fair
    Who can to me in song respond.

2. 'To steep your grass-clock plants you seek
    The pool that near the east gate lies.
  I seek that lady good and fair
    Who can with me hold converse wise.

3. 'Out to the east gate, to the moat,
    To steep your rope-rush you repair.
  Her pleasant converse to enjoy,
    I seek that lady good and fair.'
Ibid., p. 169.

The lines which follow seem to show that the lady 'good and fair' had failed to keep her appointment to meet him at the eastern gate, though the poor fellow waited from sunset to sunrise:

1. 'Where grow the willows at the eastern gate,
    And 'neath their leafy shade we could recline,
  She said at evening she would me await,
    And brightly now I see the day-star shine.

2. 'Here where the willows near the eastern gate
    Grow, and their dense leaves make a shady gloom,
  She said at evening she would me await—
    See now the morning-star the sky illume !'
Ibid., p. 169.

References to God are few and far between, but there are a few under the name of Ti (Ruler, or God) or Thien (Heaven). We give one or two verses:

> 'Oh! great is God. His glance on earth He bent,
>   Scanning our regions with severe intent
>   For one whose rule the people would content.
>   He found one T'ae.
>
> 'When this wise chieftain God to Chow had given,
>   The Kwan hordes fled away, by terror driven,
>   And sons came from the wife T'ae got from heaven.'
>   *Shi King*, p. 295.

In time of famine they prayed:

> 'Oh, pitying Heaven, why see we Thee
>   In terror thus arrayed?
>   Famine has come. The people flee,
>   And homeless roam, dismayed.
>   In settled spots, and far and near,
>   Our regions all lie waste and drear.'
>   *Ibid.*, p. 348.

References to sacrifice are rare, but the following is interesting. King Wan is associated with God, as Dr. Legge says, because through him blessings were bestowed on Chow.

> 1. 'My offerings here are given,
>   A ram, a bull.
>   Accept them, mighty Heaven,
>   All bountiful.
>
> 2. 'Thy statutes, O great King,
>   I keep, I love,
>   So on the realm to bring
>   Peace from above.
>
> 3. 'From Wan comes blessing rich;
>   Now on the right
>   He owns those gifts to which
>   Him I invite.

> 4. 'Do I not night and day
>   Revere great Heaven,
>   That thus its favours may
>   To Chow be given?'
>   *Shi King*, p. 354.

Although women are sometimes referred to in terms of disparagement, we find them occupying positions which imply the happiest relations to their husbands, and even assisting in acts of worship. The following, faithfully rendered in broad Scotch, reminds us of 'Tak yer auld cloak about ye':

> 'Says our gudewife, "The cock is crowing."
> Quoth our gudeman, "The day is dawning."
> "Get up, gudeman, and tak a spy;
> See gin the mornin' star be high,
> Syne tak' a saunter roon' aboot,
> There's rowth o' dyukes and geese to shoot;
> Lat flee and bring them hame to me,
> An' sic' a dish as ye shall pree.'
>   Etc., etc., etc.

The wife is often described as lamenting the absence of her husband, and longing for his return. The following describes the feeling of the wife of a high officer about the eleventh century before Christ:

> 1. 'Still chirp the insects in the grass,
>   All about the hoppers spring:
>   While I my husband do not see,
>   Sorrow must my bosom wring.
>   Oh, to meet him!
>   Oh, to greet him!
>   Then my heart would rest and sing.

* * * * *

3. 'Ascending high that southern hill,
    Spinous ferns I sought to find:
While I my husband do not see,
    Rankles sorrow in my mind.
        Oh, to meet him!
        Oh, to greet him!
    In my heart would peace be shrined.'

'FILIAL AFFECTION.

'Father, from whose loins I sprung,
Mother, on whose breast I hung,
Tender were ye, and ye fed,
Now upheld, now gently led.
Eyes untiring watched my way,
Often in your arms I lay.
How could I repay your love,
Vast as arch of heaven above?'

'TRUSTING GOD IN DARK TIMES.

'Where the forest once grew, we look, and, behold!
    Fagots only and twilight are left.
To Heaven, 'midst their perils, the people all look,
    And, lo! Heaven seems of reason bereft.
But is Heaven so dark? When its purpose is fixed,
    To its will opposition is vain,
And good is the rule, supreme the great God:
    He hates none of the children of men.'

The 'Yih King,' or 'Book of Changes,' seems to be an attempt to account for the mysteries of Nature by a series of diagrams which no man has ever been able to explain. It has been a delightful puzzle, over which the founders and disciples of different systems of philosophy have fought for 4,000 years, with an ingenuity and subtlety worthy of the schoolmen of the Middle Ages, and the profundity or obscurity of modern German philosophers and theologians. The theoretical

[margin: Nature of the 'Book of Changes.']

outcome has been a scepticism which anticipated Spinoza, and a practical application to divination and superstition.

The 'Book of Rites.'

The 'Li Ki,' or 'Book of Rites,' deals with the *regulation of manners* in dress, marriages, mourning, funerals, sacrifices, village feasts, etc.; forms relating to sacred places, utensils, games, etc. Confucius attached great importance to these outward forms, to which we in our day attach too little. He maintained that the outward form was the natural expression of inward feelings, which were based on virtue, and that if men neglected the outward, they would soon lose the inward feelings and the virtues from which they sprang. A favourite maxim of the sage was '*Wu puh King*,' literally rendered by Dr. Morrison, '*Never not grave*'—*i.e.*, 'always serious,' 'not in opposition to cheerfulness, but as opposed to lightness, frivolity, and hasty manners.'

The 'Chun-Tseu.'

The last of the *five classics*, the 'Chun-Tseu,' or 'Spring and Autumn,' is a bald record of events, occurring during his lifetime, written by Confucius, the only work strictly his own. All his other writings were faithful copies from ancient records, a work for which he was specially qualified.

The 'Four Books.'

The *Four Books* have been unwisely compared to our four Gospels, to which their only resemblance consists in the fact that they are chiefly records of the sayings and doings of Confucius, by four of his favourite disciples. They contain also the sayings of Mencius, who lived

200 years after Confucius, and showed a depth of thought and originality of mind superior to that of his more renowned predecessor, to whom, however, he owed much for the matter of his discourse. The disciples who compiled the greater part of the Four Books bear a much greater resemblance to Boswell, in his relation to Johnson, than the four Evangelists do to their Divine Master. They beat Boswell as gossips, and out-do the *interviewer* of the modern newspapers in England, or even of America. They and other admiring followers tell us all about their idol Confucius. Chinese Boswells.

In a previous page we have given their minute description of face and outward form as an epitome of his country. They also tell how he stood and walked and slept, the colour and cut of his clothes, and his manners in presence of his inferiors, superiors, and equals. But in spite of their many littlenesses, the outcome of excessive reverence and love, they do give us the conception of a gentle, good, and great man. Though so poor that he had to fish and shoot for his food, they tell us that he would not fish with a net nor shoot a bird when sitting on its perch. Like a true sportsman, he gave to both the chance of escape. In later years, on returning from a visit to the Emperor, he found his stables had been burned: it was noticed that he only asked if the servants had been hurt, and made no inquiry about his horses. He was faithful in every relation of life, and devout in worshipping the gods and his ancestors. He held that the virtuous and learned man was happy, though he had nothing but coarse rice to eat, rugs to cover him, and his bent elbow for a pillow, while the rich man, destitute of learning and virtue, was a miserable object of contempt.

The sayings of Confucius. The sayings of Confucius, which they have recorded with such diligence and fidelity, though often *small*, as the answers to trifling questions must be, are in general remarkable for common-sense and wisdom, and, with perhaps one or two doubtful cases, strictly moral and beneficent. The following are a few examples:

'That which is called rectifying the motives is this: Do not deceive yourself; hate vice as you do an offensive smell; love virtue as you love beauty. This is called self-enjoyment. Hence the superior man will carefully watch over his motives.'

'Adorning the person with virtue depends on rectifying the heart.'

'The proper regulation of the family depends on the cultivation of personal virtue.'

'All who hold the reins of government have nine standard rules by which to act. These require them to cultivate personal virtue, honour the virtuous, love their relations, respect great officers, consider the whole of their ministers as members of their own body, view the people as their children, encourage all the trades, treat foreigners with kindness, and manifest a tender care for tributary princes.'

'Confucius says, If you read and do not reflect, you will lose what you learn. If you think and do not study, you are uneasy and in danger.'

'Confucius says, It is only the virtuous that are capable of either loving or hating a man.'

'Confucius said, I have not seen anyone who perfectly loves virtue, nor have I seen anyone who thoroughly detests vice.'

'Confucius said, In learning I am equal to others; but I cannot by any means exhibit the man of perfect virtue in my own conduct.'

'Confucius said, Virtue consists in conquering self, and returning to propriety.' And 'WHAT YOU DO NOT WANT DONE TO YOURSELF, DO NOT TO OTHERS.' This is the Chinese sage's nearest approach to the GOLDEN RULE. It is negative in form, but is substantially the same as the rule laid down by Christ. We shall find that his contemporary, Lao-tse, went much further, and even counselled his followers to RENDER GOOD FOR EVIL.

GENERAL LITERATURE.

The general literature of China is plentiful, but **Chinese** limited in its range of subjects, and wearily **libraries.** monotonous from the constant desire to imitate or reproduce the style and treatment of the ancients.

The *catalogue* of the four libraries in Pekin consists of 112 octavo volumes, and contains 3,440 separate works, consisting of 78,000 volumes. Besides this, other catalogues of imperial libraries give lists of 6,764 works in 93,243 volumes.* The catalogues are classified under different subjects, of which the first is the text and commentaries on the *Five Classics* and the *Four Books*. They are, we are told, in many cases learned and able, but as a whole inexhaustibly wearisome, and in many cases worthless.

Second, *history* occupies a large place, and no country in the world has better materials for a good history than China. Official records are kept by competent men of the events of every reign, and every province and considerable town in China has its local *handbook* or history.

The third division is *historical novels*, of which the people are very fond. Many of these are painfully realistic and immoral, but if openly licentious the sale is prohibited by law. The law, however, is practically a dead letter; magistrates, Government clerks, and other officials, are the chief offenders in the purchase and reading of such vile trash.

Fourth, *dramatic* works are numerous, but in general, like the worse class of novels, are published under fictitious names, as being a dishonourable class of works. They are called in the Amoy dialect *siau swat*, or *small talk*.

Fifth, *poetry*, chiefly short compositions express-

* Wells Williams' 'Middle Kingdom.'

Education and Literature

ing the tender and mournful feelings, or descriptive of rural scenery.

The others, as given by Morrison, are as follows:
Sixth, *collectanea*.

Seventh, *geographical* and *topographical* works.

Eighth, books on *medicine*, which are well fitted to amuse the medical faculty of Europe, though not always useless, even to modern science.

Ninth, *astronomy*.

Tenth, *prize essays*.

And last, but not least, *moral and religious* works, by the adherents of the three religions of China.

There are two classes of works not named in this list which are a feature in Chinese literature. We know not under which class they are placed. The first, *encyclopædias*, which are found in hundreds of quarto volumes, written centuries before such works were dreamed of in the West; and second, *dictionaries*, some of them composed at the commencement of the Christian era. That of Kang-hi, in the seventeenth century, was prepared at his order by 700 learned men, and superintended by himself. It consists of 138 thick volumes, and is worthy of the great monarch who planned it and published it at the expense of the Government. This dictionary, translated in an abridged form by Dr. Morrison, and published by the East India Company in six quarto volumes, contains, he tells us, 43,496 characters, or, as we may say, *words:*

[margin: Encyclopædias and dictionaries.]

In the body of the work	31,214 characters.
Added, principally obsolete or incorrect	6,423 ,,
Not found in any previous dictionary	1,659 ,,
Without names or meaning	4,200 ,,

Such a formidable list of uncouth characters might well deter any ordinary scholar from the study of such a language; but, happily, the number required for ordinary use is limited to comparatively few. The whole of the Penal Code of China is written in a simple style, so as to be understood by any scholar, and contains only 2,000 different characters. The nine canonical classical works contain only 4,600 *different* characters, although the number by repetition runs up to more than 200,000 in the five classics, and the other four books would add greatly to the number. With a knowledge of 5,000 characters a man would be a good scholar; with 2,000 he could get on creditably.

China's Augustan age. The Augustan age of the modern literature of China was during the Tang dynasty—the ninth and tenth centuries of the Christian era, the darkest age in European letters. It was renowned for its poets, of whom Li Tai-peh and Su Tung-pi are said to have been the most famous. If we may judge of their quality by the quantity of their productions, they will throw the poets of Europe into the shade. Li's poems fill 30 volumes, and those of Su 115. The collected poems of the Tang dynasty have been published by imperial authority in 900 volumes. The proportion of descriptive poetry in it is small compared with the sentimental. The longest poem yet turned into English is the 'Hwa Tsien Ki,' or 'The Flower's Petal,' by P. P. Thoms. Another of much greater repute among native scholars, called 'Li Sao,' or 'Dissipation of Sorrows,' dating from about 314 years before Christ, has been rendered into French by 'D'Hervey-Saint-Denys.' We give from the above the following specimen of poetry from Dr. W. Williams' 'Middle Kingdom.'

The description of the home-sickness, caused by playing plaintively some familiar old tune, recalls the effect produced by the bagpipes on Highland soldiers in India, when intercourse was rare and service long. It did not lead to desertion, but to physical prostration, and had to be discontinued.

'CHANG LIANG'S FLUTE.

' 'Twas night : the tired soldiers were peacefully sleeping,
  The low hum of voices was hushed in repose,
The sentries in silence their strict watch were keeping
  'Gainst surprise, or a sudden attack of their foes,

' When a low mellow note on the night-air came stealing :
  So soothingly over the senses it fell,
So touchingly sweet, so soft and appealing,
  Like the musical tones of an aerial bell.

  * * * * * *

' The sleepers arouse, and with beating hearts listen.
  In their dreams they had heard that weird music before ;
It touches each heart, with tears their eyes glisten,
  For it tells them of those they may never see more.

  * * * * * *

'Each looked at the other, but no word was spoken,
　　The music insensibly tempting them on :
They *must* hasten home.　Ere the daylight had broken,
　　The enemy looked, and, behold ! they were gone.

'There's a magic in music, a witchery in it,
　　Indescribable either with tongue or with pen.
The flute of Chang Liang, in one little minute
　　Had stolen the courage of eight thousand men.'

CHAPTER VI.

THE RELIGION OF CHINA.

NO form of religious worship comes so near **Primitive religion.** to what we have good reason to believe was the cultus of the primitive founders of the human race, as that of the Chinese. The form of worship among the Jews was changed on their departure from Egypt from the patriarchal to the national. The religious worship of the Babylonians and Egyptians, which were as ancient as that of China, perished with these old empires long ago. The present rites of the Hindus are of comparatively recent origin, while the religious customs of the Greeks and Romans, which only existed for a few centuries during their classic supremacy, were borrowed from the East, and perished before the advancing light of Christianity. But China, in this nineteenth century of the Christian era, holds fast the same religion, and practises the same religious rites, as those of Noah, if not the same as those of Adam and his immediate descendants.*

* I make no apology for taking the Mosaic account of the origin of religion as the only true and consistent one. I

The one religion of China. Many will be surprised at our speaking of the religion of China as *one;* the universal custom is to speak of the *three* religions of China, which are called Confucianism, Taoism, and Buddhism. We object to both the number and the nomenclature. If we profess to enumerate all the religions which have been accepted by a large number of the inhabitants of China, and that have received Government sanction, and some even imperial patronage, they would be at least thrice three; but if we look carefully into the three great forms of religion we have named, we shall find that there is only one that is indigenous to China, which forms the real national religion, namely, that commonly called Confucianism.

Not Confucianism. We object, however, to the term 'Confucian religion.' Confucius never professed to be the founder of a religion; he laid no claim to the character of a religious teacher. He called himself a *transmitter*. His great work was to discover the most ancient form of belief and practice in all departments of political, moral, social, and religious life. He wrote in the sixth century before Christ—a century noted for its great religious movements both in the eastern and western hemispheres, a century which produced such reformers as Buddha in India, Zoroaster in

---

hope to demonstrate this ere long. Indeed, our ablest students of comparative religions are beginning to despair of all other inventions—as varied as they are vain, and mutually destructive.

Persia, Ezra in Babylon and Jerusalem, and Pythagoras in Greece—a wave of religious reform which circled the world—a Divine reformation which did much to save the world from moral and religious corruption and decay. Of all the great men of that remarkable period, none exerted so wide and lasting an influence as Confucius. Four hundred millions now own the sway of that 'uncrowned king of men,' and though his influence is detrimental when the old empire comes in contact, or into conflict, with modern civilization, there is no doubt that the teaching of Confucius developed a form of mental and material culture in the largest empire in the world, and has preserved it in independence and prosperity far longer than any that has ever been united in one land—speaking one language, obeying one law, and practising one form of religious worship.

Confucius, we have seen, professed to be a *transmitter*, but what was it he did transmit to his contemporaries and to posterity? He tells us plainly and repeatedly that his great mission —for he felt he had a *mission*—was to transmit the knowledge and wisdom of the great Emperors Yao and Shun, with whom he maintained authentic history began. Not that these were the first men, or even the first Emperors, of China; he knew that there were authentic traditions of a much earlier period, but his practical, matter-of-fact mind would not transmit

Confucius' work.

anything for which he had not authentic documentary evidence. Traditions and myths had their own place, but they were not *history*, and were kept apart from his historic works.

Commencement of history.

This commencement of history in China, as we have seen, dated from the twenty-third century before Christ, 600 years before Moses; but both Moses and the Emperor Yao had knowledge, either in the form of oral or written traditions, of a much earlier period. In all probability they had both forms of tradition. There is abundant evidence in both Eastern and Western Asia that the art of writing was known from a very early period. The traditions of Babylon, Egypt, and China are substantially at one in making the discovery of letters to have taken place about the same period, and that is as early as about 3,000 years before Christ. Some date the commencement of authentic history from the reign of the Emperor Fuhi, who flourished 2,800 years before Christ. We prefer to regard it as the beginning of written traditions—the materials for history.

What the religion was.

But what, we shall be asked, was the religion believed in and practised in the days of Yao and Shun, which they professed to have received from a much more remote period than the twenty-third century before Christ, in which they flourished? The answer is easy and conclusive. It was substantially the same as that which is the formal creed and practice of the Chinese of the present day in their natural worship. The worship of the Emperor of China in this nineteenth century is the same as that of the Emperors of the Ming dynasty in the fourteenth century; and we are assured on historic evidence, that when the peasant founder of that dynasty drove the Mongols out of China, he appointed a body of the most learned men in the empire to reform the religious worship which had been corrupted by the invaders, and to restore it to the form in which it was practised in the earliest times.

There is no doubt that the liturgy of the Ming dynasty, founded in the fourteenth century of our era, was the same as it was in the days of Confucius in the sixth century before Christ, and Confucius made it his aim to render the worship of his time the same as it was in the days of Yao and Shun, in the twenty-third century before Christ. But these venerable sages scrupulously adhered to the religious customs handed down from a much earlier period. Thus, by well-marked stages, we can easily retrace our steps back in the footprints of history, from the present to the most primitive period of religious worship known to us—the patriarchal, when the father of the family, or head of the tribe, was the priest, and offered the sacrifice and the public prayers for all the family or tribe.

What, then, is the present religion of China, which we may accept as substantially the same as *Present and past religion of China.*

that of the earliest? Before we answer that question we must show briefly the mutual relation of the three forms of religion which are so generally practised, and how the two subordinate forms stand related to that which we call the one indigenous religion of China.

From the earliest times until the first century of the Christian era there was no doubt about the unity of the religion of China. No form of religion was recognised, except that which had been handed down from the most remote antiquity. Heresies did arise, but they were short-lived and of limited extent, and with the sacred classics in the hands of the people, reformers, like Luther, could always appeal to the universally-accepted authority of the *Sacred Books*. So strong was this feeling, that when the despot Chi, who revolutionized the government, wished to perpetuate his corruption in both civil and sacred things, he ordered all the ancient classics to be burned, and the scholars who had committed them to memory to be put to death. But such was the love of the people for these Sacred Books, that even he failed, and the religion of the country was restored to its old form after his death.

THE RELIGION OF LAOTSZE.

<small>The reputed founder of Taoism.</small> The reputed founder of Taoism, Laotsze, had no religion but that of the ancient sages of China —the same as his contemporary, Confucius. He

never attempted either to form a religion of his own or to alter the ancestral religion. He was a devout old mystic, who philosophized on the mysteries of the old religion, and gave utterance to sentiments of profound depth and great moral beauty. He not only taught, as Confucius did, that 'we should not do to others what we would not wish others to do to us'—the negative side of the Golden Rule as taught by Christ—but he went the full length of teaching in China the higher law, *to render good for evil*, 500 years before it was laid down by the *Great Teacher* in Judæa.

Christ's originality did not consist in the substance of His teaching, but in its *power*, derived from His Divine authority, and His practice of what He taught. Moses, Buddha, Confucius, and Laotsze all taught the same great ethical truths long before the advent of Him who was the true Light of the world. These old sages were taught by Him who gave them that moral nature and intellectual power by which they could arrive at the highest ideals far above their moral practice; if not derived from Divine traditions.

While Laotsze adhered to the old religion, he introduced speculations about the doctrine of the *Tao*, in which the early sages had indulged centuries before, and the possibility of prolonging life indefinitely, which led his followers to superstitious rites, and to engage in the vain search after the philosopher's stone and the elixir of immortality. Laotsze sought to prolong life by a regulated

Laotsze's speculations.

moral conduct, but his followers tried to secure it by material means, and anticipated the alchemists of Europe by well-nigh 2,000 years. But all this was outside of religion, and did not interfere with conformity with the old faith and ceremonials of the national religion. It was the followers of Laotsze who copied from the rites and superstitions of a corrupted Buddhism, and formed themselves into a kind of religious sect, and became what they are now—a body of superstitious demon-worshippers, with a graduated priesthood in gaudy vestments, and an elaborate ritual, practising all kinds of geomancy and necromancy, in utter defiance of the spirit and teaching of their nominal founder.

<small>Buddhism a foreign religion.</small> Buddhism was introduced from India into China in the year 66 A.D. by an imperial deputation sent in search of a sage reported to have appeared in the West. Some have supposed it was the Christ of whose advent a rumour had reached China. As a system of transcendental philosophy of religion, it would require a volume to give a just account of its true character, and of the wonderful character of the man who founded it. We should be sorry to do injustice to a character so beautiful and so philanthropic. There is little necessity for making the attempt; the form of Buddhism which was introduced into China 500 years after his death was so corrupted and disguised that it is difficult to see its connection with the creed and customs of its founder.

Buddha was a philosophical atheist, and an agnostic in regard to the future state; but his followers have made him a supreme deity, and have surrounded him with thousands of demigods. Buddha was the great enemy of superstition and of rites and ceremonies; the religion of his successors is the most superstitious and ritualistic of all the religions of the world, except it be the Roman Catholic, to which it bears a most striking resemblance. Buddha had no true place for prayer; the priests of Buddhism spend much of their time in repeating prayers in an unknown tongue, and have reduced the system to a mechanical process, employing revolving drums, windmills, and water-wheels to repeat their supplications; and, by an irony of fate, the endless repetition of the name of their atheistic founder is supposed to be the most effectual in securing salvation, which Buddha declared could only be obtained by the meritorious works of the individual. *[Corruptions of Buddhism.]*

It was this corrupted and degraded form of Buddhism which was introduced into China in the first century. Some learned and earnest seekers after truth were able, we doubt not, from the study of Buddhist literature, to get some idea of the nobler aims and sentiments of the great Indian reformer; but the great mass of the people saw in Buddhism nothing but the superstitions and idolatry and gaudy forms which satisfied a craving for something positive and external, for which the *[Corrupted form introduced into China.]*

patriarchal worship provided no nourishment. It was something they could accept without forsaking or dissenting from the old religion. This is the general attitude towards the Buddhist religion in China. It has no power to elevate the souls of the worshippers. The majority of the people who use its rites speak of it with contempt, and despise the priests or monks as ignorant and idle fellows, who are of no use to the community or the State. As for the literati, they frequently publish tracts denouncing the idolatry and useless rites of the Buddhists in unmeasured terms.

<small>Mutual relations of the three religions.</small> The mutual relations of the three forms of religion in China are of the most friendly character. They are not antagonistic to one another. They have formed an alliance, based, on the one hand, on a frigid religious indifference, and on the other by their being supplementary to one another.

Buddhism—a foreign importation—altered the entire system of Taoism, which adopted much of the popular ecclesiastical system, and copied many of the rites and customs of Buddhism. So much is this the case, that it is difficult for a stranger to distinguish the temples of the one from those of the other religion. There are as many gods in those of the one as in those of the other, and they have a family likeness, with little but a change of names. The three principal gods of a Buddhist temple are called the three *precious ones*, those in a Taoist temple are the three *pure ones*, and both temples are filled with a host of subordinate deities or demons, while the priests or monks are much alike in costume, and rites, and ceremonies. Those of the Taoists are obviously borrowed from Buddhists, while there is little doubt that the Buddhists have been influenced in their turn by the beliefs and rites of the Taoists.

The marvellous circumstance is that the old patriarchal worship has been preserved almost entirely free from the influences of either Taoism or Buddhism. It remains the same as it was long before the rise of the corrupt form of Taoism after the death of Laotsze. It is a strong proof of the powerful hold the patriarchal religion had got of the hearts of the people, and the firm root it had taken in the constitution and custom of the empire. Nothing could have given it such a hold and such a sense of its inviolable sanctity but the fact of its great antiquity, and the conviction of its sacred origin, which makes modern innovations of human origin inadmissible and profane. *Preservation of patriarchal religion.*

The work of Confucius in making up the Canon of sacred books must have had the same effect in securing the permanence of the religion of China that the formation of the Canon of the Old Testament in the time of Ezra had on the religion of the Jews, and which the fixing of the Canon of the New Testament had on the Creed and form of the Christian Church. In fact, the influence of the *The Chinese Canon.*

Confucian Classics and Analects has given a more fixed and unyielding form to the religion of the Chinese than the formation of the Canon of Scripture has given to the religion of Christians.

Tolerance of Chinese religion. But while the patriarchal religion of China remains thus intact, and comparatively uncorrupted, it has sanctioned the introduction of Buddhism and the corruptions of Taoism. It is so tolerant as to allow of their being not only practised by the people, but recognised, and even patronized, by the State. The same man may be what is commonly called by foreign writers *a thorough Confucianist*, and yet a devout worshipper in the temples of the Taoists and Buddhists. Even Emperors, who acted in their official capacity as high-priests in the patriarchal rites and sacrifices, have been leaders in Taoist superstitious practices, and some were devout Buddhists. As for the great mass of the people, they practise all the three forms of worship, and at all the great events of social and domestic life, the man who would call himself a follower of the old faith would think himself quite consistent in calling in the priests or monks of Taoism and Buddhism to perform their ceremonies at the birth, the burial, or marriage of his sons and daughters, and the ministers of these two different sects would see no impropriety in the union of their diverse rites. The frigid creed of Confucius is not incompatible with their introduction.

This is not an incongruity confined to the

religion of China. Almost all false religions tolerate others, so long as that toleration is compatible with adherence to their own creed and form; it is only when the adoption of the new involves the rejection of the old that they oppose and persecute. This is the more true when religion becomes a lifeless form. Such tolerance is incompatible with earnestness in the belief and pursuit of the true and the Divine. Christianity is the most intolerant of all religions, and rightly so, because of the divinity of its origin and the importance of its creed and worship. It teaches tolerance towards the liberty of those who follow other religions, but it admits of no incorporation of the faith and practices of other religions with its own. Christ's maxim was, 'He that is not with Me is against Me.' "No man can serve two masters.' *[False tolerance. True intolerance.]*

What, then, is the true religion of China, which we find so free from the innovation of imported Buddhism and the corruptions of Taoism? The answer must be brief. *[Chinese henotheism.]*

First of all, the creed is what may be called *henotheistic*.* The supreme object of worship is One, but he is attended by subordinate deities, or deified ancestors or heroes, who receive a lower form of worship, and are regarded as attendants on the Supreme God, who is worshipped with the highest honours. When the Emperor *invites* the

* We do not use this term in the sense attached to it by Professor Max Müller, but as here defined.

deity to come to the altar, he *summons* the others as his attendants.

This supreme object of worship is known by the names or titles of *Ti* (Ruler), or *Shang-ti* (Supreme Ruler), or *Thien* (Heaven), the name by which God was designated in the earliest times, and found in use by Nebuchadnezzar in Babylon, and applied by Daniel to the God of Israel : ' until thou know that the heavens do rule.' The use of the term *heaven* for God as the great *Ruler*, is quite in harmony with the Chinese conception. The name of the dwelling-place of God is used for that of its great Occupant as not only appropriate in itself, but as more reverent than the personal name.

<small>The Divine attributes.</small>
The attributes of Shang-ti are summed up by Dr. Medhurst, Dr. Faber, and other competent authorities in such terms as the following: ' Shang-ti made the heaven, and the earth, and man. He is the true Parent of all things. His love is over all his works. He is the great and lofty One, whose dominion is everlasting. His years are without end. His goodness is infinite. Spirits and men are alike under his government.'

'This,' Dr. Medhurst adds, 'is what China holds, and, in her highest exercise of devotion, declares concerning Shang-ti. I am confident the Christian world will agree with me in saying, " This God is our God." '

This might be called *monotheism*, were it not that the word signifies not only the worship of one

God, but the *entire exclusion* of all other objects of worship, even of an inferior kind. We prefer to call it *henotheism*, which implies, in the sense in which we use the term, the worship of one Supreme God, but does not exclude the worship of other gods subordinate to the *One*. We do not know of any heathen religion which has risen to the true conception of monotheistic worship, though several have attained to the conception, or retained the memory of the worship of one God as supreme over all other gods. Some of the inferior deities worshipped in the great sacrifices of the national religion of China are, as given by Wells Williams, the sky and earth, the Temple of Ancestors, and the gods of land and grain. Others are honoured by *medium* and *inferior* sacrifices, but these are offered by the Emperor's subordinates.

Along with this faith in God, the patriarchal religion teaches the doctrine of a future state of rewards for good men, but says little about the punishment of the wicked. The sacrifice of animal life was, in its original significance, an acknowledgment of sin and of the forgiveness of sin through the offering of a substitute.

Of this simple and comparatively pure faith, the Emperor of China is the representative head and pontiff. There is in the ancient religion of China no priestly class. The Emperor is the representative of, and the only priest of, the nation. He keeps up the form of worship

The Emperor the only priest and worshipper of Shang-ti.

designed originally for the patriarchal head of the family or tribe, as father of the largest empire in the world, an abuse of the Divine institution meant only for the infancy of the world, and abolished at the exodus of the Israelites from Egypt. The effect is disastrous to the religion of the people. The Emperor alone can approach the Supreme God by prayer and sacrifice. The officers of State and governors of the provinces worship subordinate deities, and the body of the people must worship their ancestors, but no one except the Emperor may presume to worship the Supreme God—Shang-ti or Thien.

Injurious effect on the people. The consequence is that ancestor-worship is the only national worship of the people of China. This is the chief reason why they add to their old and indigenous religion the creeds and worship of the Buddhists and Taoists, as a supplement to the defective faith and form of that which they still cling to as the true religion of their fathers of old time. There are few Chinamen who would call themselves Taoists or Buddhists. The great majority—we may say almost all, except the lowest of the people—hold both Taoism and Buddhism and their priests in contempt, even when using their service as supplementary of their own. Superficial writers and admirers talk of the 300 or 400 millions of Buddhists in China —a most absurd estimate. The men who know China best declare that not more than 30,000,000 or 40,000,000 in the whole of China proper would

The Religion of China

call themselves Buddhists, if a religious census of the people were taken.

The national form of worship is most impressive and interesting as a relic of the primitive worship of the early patriarchs, so far as known from the earliest records of the Jewish Scriptures and Chinese classics. It is only once or twice in the year that the Emperor, as father and priest of the nation, approaches Shang-ti: at the spring and autumn solstices, the former being the more important and invariable, connected as it is with the opening labours of the year, when the Emperor ploughs a furrow, and his courtiers an increasing number, according as they descend in rank, as an example of industry to the people; while the Empress goes with her attendants into the mulberry-groves to feed the silkworms, as an encouragement to females in the production of silk, which has, as a manufacture, flourished in China from the earliest historic period. *[Form of worship.]*

The solemn day of sacrifice is preceded by a period of fasting, and the Emperor spends the night alone in a humble dwelling near the place of sacrifice, to prepare himself for his solemn duties. The Sacred Books declare that if the heart is not purified the sacrifices and prayers will not be accepted.

Some time before, the animals for sacrifice are carefully inspected by high officials of the Board of Sacred Rites, to see that they are perfect in form and colour, and are in good condition. The *[The victims and temple.]*

distinction between clean and unclean has long been lost, and animals of all kinds are used in sacrifice: the horse as well as the ox, the sow as well as the sheep. The victims are all slain and prepared the day before by butchers with whom no idea of priesthood is associated. Among the Jews, also, anyone could kill the animals offered in sacrifice.

On the day prescribed in the imperial almanac, which is prepared yearly by the astronomical bureau attached to the Board of Rites, the Emperor, attended by the highest officials of the Government, approaches an *altar of earth*, such as we find prescribed in the twentieth chapter of Exodus. It stands in the open air, under the canopy of heaven—Nature's grandest temple— with no image of any kind. Only on a table near stand the ancestral tablets of the dynasty, with the names of the Emperor's predecessors. The sacrifices, consisting of the bodies of the slain beasts, along with gifts of silks and gems, with libations of wine, are duly presented, while prayers are offered to Shang-ti, or Thien, as a living person—the hearer of prayer—and hymns are sung by a choir playing on instruments of peculiar construction and great antiquity of form. A solemn rite. The demeanour of the Emperor is the extreme of humility. The man who will not allow the highest of his 400,000,000 of subjects to approach him without the lowest and most humiliating prostration, now prostrates himself nine times, again

The Religion of China

and again striking his forehead in the dust before this invisible but real object of his worship; and this he does as prescribed in the ritual, and after the example of the ancient Emperors Yao and Shun, who acknowledged it to be much more ancient. It may have been derived from Fuh-hi, who flourished nearly 3,000 years before Christ; and by him from others of earlier date.

The following prayer we quote from Dr. Legge's translation in his ' Notions of the Chinese concerning God and Spirits.' He tells us it was used up to the time of the Emperor Keu-tsing in the sixteenth century, who then altered *one word*, changing *Haou* (bright) into *Hwang* (sovereign) as applied to the heavens. Even this is noticed by the Chinese as an innovation. 'To Thee, O mysteriously-working Maker, I look up in thought. How imperial is the expansive arch (where Thou dwellest)! Now is the time when the masculine energies of Nature begin to be displayed, and with the greater ceremonies I reverently honour Thee. I, Thy servant, am but a reed or willow; my heart is but as that of an ant; yet have I received Thy favouring decree, appointing me to the government of the empire. I deeply cherish a sense of my ignorance and blindness, and am afraid lest I prove unworthy of Thy great favour. Therefore will I observe all the rules and statutes, striving, insignificant as I am, to discharge my loyal duty. Far distant here, I look up to Thy heavenly palace. Come in Thy precious chariot to the altar. Thy

A prayer said by the Emperor.

servant, I bow my head to the earth, reverently expecting Thine abundant grace. All my officers are here arranged along with me, joyfully worshipping Thee. All the spirits accompany Thee as guards, (filling the air) from the east to the west. Thy servant, I prostrate myself before Thee, and reverently look up for Thy coming. O Ti (Ruler), O that Thou wouldst vouchsafe to accept our offerings, and regard us, while thus we worship Thee, whose goodness is inexhaustible.'

<small>Hymns from the Chinese liturgy.</small> We give two or three of the hymns or psalms that are sung by the choir. They are only fair samples of many others:

'When Ti (God) the Lord had so decreed, He called into existence heaven, earth, and men. Between (heaven and earth) He separately disposed men and all things, all overspread by the heavens. I, His unworthy servant, beg His (favouring) decree to enlighten me, His minister—so may I ever appear before Him in the empyrean.'

This very literal rendering may be turned, with an equally literal, but very rude, imitation of Sir Francis Rouse's version of the Psalms of David, to show the resemblance between the sacred songs of China and Palestine in those early times, the Chinese being the older of the two.

'When God the Lord made heaven and earth,
　By His supreme decree
He men and all things placed between,
　Beneath heaven's canopy.

'May He unto His servant grant
　Light for my ministry,
That I may dwell for evermore
　Before His face on high.'

The following hymn is sung at the last offering of wine:

'The precious feast is wide displayed, the generous benches are arranged, the pearly wine is presented with music and dances. The spirit of harmony is collected; men and creatures are happy. The breast of Thy servant is troubled, lest he be unable to express his obligations.'

At the removal of the offerings they sing:

'The service of song is completed, but our poor sincerity cannot be expressed. Thy sovereign goodness is infinite. As a potter hast Thou made all things. Great and small are sheltered (by Thy love). As engraven on the heart of Thy poor servant is the sense of Thy goodness, so that my feelings cannot be fully displayed. With great kindness Thou dost bear with us, and, notwithstanding our demerit, dost grant us life and prosperity.'

Such is a brief and imperfect description of the true and only religion of the Chinese as a nation. Taoism, as taught by Taotsze, was, as we have seen, essentially the same as conceived of by a pure-minded old mystic. His teaching was as much in harmony with the ancient religion handed down by Confucius as the teaching of Madame Guyon, Jacob Behmen, and William Law was in general harmony with the New Testament.

There are comparatively few Chinese who would call themselves Taoists, as distinct from, or opposed to, the followers of the patriarchal religion—perhaps not more than would call themselves Buddhists, a number which is placed by some authorities as low as 20,000,000 in China proper. Both are but fractions of the vast empire which is so deeply imbued with the old patriarchal religion of the country.

Free from cruel and licentious rites. It adds greatly to our appreciation of the religion of China that it has never been profaned or polluted by cruel and licentious rites, like the religions of almost, if not all, other countries. There is not a word or rite to cause a shudder, or raise a blush, in the most sensitive mind; and this is true of the whole of its history from the very earliest times. No human victim ever bled on a Chinese altar of the national religion, although the practice prevailed among the rude aborigines of the country. No temple in China was ever polluted by the excesses practised in the temples of ancient Greece and Rome, and which now prevail in India. No idol ever insulted the majesty of the infinite and invisible God. No hero of cruel or immoral character was ever raised to the rank of even a demigod. A Baal, or Jupiter, or Thor would be abhorrent to Chinese ideas of deity. As for a Dionysus, a Bacchus, or a Krishna; an Astarte, an Aphrodite, or a Venus, they would not only be expelled with horror from the outer courts of a national temple: they would be excluded from the precincts of the meanest Buddhist or Taoist shrine in China.

While we find pleasure in giving expression to our high estimate of the primitive simplicity and purity of the real religion of China, and to the beauty of its ancient liturgy, we are far from being blind to its many defects and faults, which it would be easy to point out; but this is no part of our plan. These will be dealt with in another work which we hope to issue ere long, in which the religion of China will be more fully discussed, and compared with other religions. We leave it as imperfectly but truthfully portrayed, a most valuable relic of primitive religion, unequalled by any save that of the Jewish and Christian Scriptures. With the early tradition of the former it wonderfully agrees, and confirms its credibility. This confirmation of the old Mosaic records is the more remarkable and convincing from the Chinese creed and worship being now offered in ignorance of their true significance. The faith and worship, though honest and earnest, are not the expression of truths arrived at by intellectual and religious conviction. They are held and practised from respect for the truths handed down from remote antiquity — truths accepted on historic evidence and the authority of venerated ancestors.

In the present day, and even in the age of Confucius, the true significance of the worship of Shang-ti was unknown. Confucius himself confessed that he knew nothing of the meaning of the imperial sacrifices; yet he attended them with the greatest reverence, and severely censured those who attended them with an air of indifference. They are the stereotyped creed and worship of the world in its primitive simplicity, and are as deserving of our respect as they are of the reverence of the Chinese.

CHAPTER VII.

THE FUTURE OF CHINA.

China's position. WITHOUT attempting to predict a definite future for China, or dogmatizing on the effect of modern civilization on her political, commercial and social life, it may be well to give a few reasons for taking a hopeful view of the destiny of that vast and venerable empire, and to give some reasons why foreign nations should not attempt to use physical force to accomplish rational and moral results which can only be realized by intelligent and voluntary convictions; and to help so far as we can to put an end to the foolish talk of the absorption of China by some one European Power, or the division of the country among a number of mutually jealous and antagonistic empires.

Our reasons for hopefulness as to the future independence and material and moral progress of China are found under the preceding chapters of our book, and we trust to the inferences being drawn by our readers; but for greater clearness and helpfulness we may briefly state our own convictions.

We assume that China cannot proceed on the old lines now that she has been so rudely awakened out of her long sleep. The leading minds in China are now alive to the necessity for introducing the scientific and mechanical appliances by which she has been so repeatedly humbled in recent wars; especially as this has been demonstrated in the sudden rise to power of her little old dependency, Japan. *China awaking.*

The evidences of this awakening are manifold. The most hopeful is the establishment by the Government of a college in Peking, under the presidency of an American missionary, who has for years been on the best of terms with the leading members of the Tsungli Yamen. The introduction for some years past of questions outside the books of Confucius is a great innovation on old Chinese notions, and the premature attempt of the young Emperor to make an entire and immediate revolution in these examinations shows how the leaven is working, and, though overturned by the usurpation of the old Empress, the change is inevitable in the near future. This breaking with the past in such an ancient and fundamental institution has an importance and significance which the foreigner can hardly understand.

This change in education and in the examinations for office is much more important than the competitive examinations in our Civil Service, which *Education movement.*

do not include in this country, as in China, admission to the office of Prime Minister and of Secretaries of State for all departments of the Government, and has given a new impulse and direction to education all over the country. The Chinese are now establishing high schools in many cities of the Empire, and sending their children to the schools of missionaries in large numbers, to be taught the learning of Europe, and to a large extent in the English tongue. They are so convinced of the advantages of this education that they willingly pay for their instruction, and regard it as a good investment, now more profitable than the old style. This is accompanied by a demand for books on scientific subjects, and the presses of missionary societies are kept busy printing such works as have been translated into the Chinese language.

Effect of the Japanese War. Since the recent war there has been a great increase in the number, and greater intelligence in the inquirers after Christian teaching and Christian books. It is not merely that men seek such knowledge for the salvation of their souls, but because they feel that there must be something in the religion which endows these Christian nations with such resistless power, and the means of acquiring such wealth. The rapid rise of Japan has helped much to spread this spirit of inquiry. It has brought the subject before the minds of the Chinese far more forcibly. They know who and what the Japanese are, and that a paltry island, which had borrowed all its literature and art from China, and had until recently been a small dependency of the empire, should, by copying the arts and sciences of Christian nations, suddenly become more than a match in warfare and enterprise for all the power of the 'Middle Kingdom,' seemed a miracle, and showed that there was a mysterious power which had to be reckoned with, unknown to Confucius, and not revealed in the sacred records of Yao and Shun. Happily, this spirit of inquiry, when awakened by secular facts, frequently leads to spiritual results. The number of Christian converts since the Japanese War has very largely increased.

The great extension of commercial enterprise by the Chinese of late years, the increase of emigration, not merely, as of old, to the Straits of Malacca, but to distant regions and civilized countries, the opening up of the central provinces to steam navigation and foreign trade, the concession to the laying down of telegraph and railway lines, and the opening of mines, though granted reluctantly under external pressure, will make a return to the slumber of the past impossible. Even phlegmatic China cannot sleep with the click of the telegraph, the whistle of the railways, and the scream of the steamboat in her ears. The awakening may not yet be complete; it may take some more shaking by external powers, perhaps even some blows from the 'mailed fist.' A giant who has slept for centuries takes

Sleep now impossible.

time to stretch himself and rub his eyes, but when thoroughly aroused, his march will be to the front of Asiatic progress in the future, as it has been for thousands of years in the past.

GROUNDS FOR HOPE.

<small>Extent and unity of China.</small> We find the first ground of hopefulness for the future of China in the country itself. When people speak of breaking up the Empire of China, or the conquest of it by any one nation in Europe, they forget what the empire is. A country of 1,800 miles in length, and as much in breadth, a compact and solid unity, of ample resources for a population equal to the fourth part of the whole world, a population of one race, one law, one national religion, from which there is almost no dissent, only additions—to break up such a country into portions to suit the limited capacity of assimilation by the small nations of Europe would be a hard task if the nations of Europe were of one mind, but with their suspicions and jealousies, impossible, and likely to lead to endless wars, both in Asia and Europe; to swallow it whole would be found to be an indigestible meal by the largest.

It took England a century to conquer India, a country divided into a hundred petty States, separated by many distinct races, of different languages and laws and antagonistic religions, constantly at war with one another, where the maxim 'Divide and conquer' was comparatively easy. China is a united nation, and though it could be overrun, it would be very difficult to subdue, as will be seen from its history. The self-satisfied exclusiveness of China is excusable in view of its vastness, compactness, and completeness of resources for all the wants of the population. Now that it is about to enter the comity of civilized empires, it will be found capable of maintaining its unity and independence if only given fair play by juvenile—one might say upstart—nationalities which have got the start in the race for civilization while China was handicapped by its unwieldy bulk and venerable prejudices.

Our second ground of hopefulness is derived from a study of the history of China. Her past and present civilization is, as we have seen, all her own; she owes nothing but her misfortunes to foreign sources. A nation that could originate so much that is good in the industries and inventions, the laws, government, and administration of so vast an empire is not likely to be broken to pieces or swallowed up by any external power. Macaulay said of the Spaniards that 'they were easily defeated, but very difficult to conquer.' This is much more true of China. During the 4,000 years of her history China has *never been conquered*. She has been twice defeated and overrun by external enemies, but not conquered; not a law, nor social custom, nor form of religion, was changed. The greatest change ever effected by a victorious invader was that of wearing the hair

The past inspires hope.

long instead of short, and to impose this contemptible custom of wearing a queue cost the Tartars years of bloody war; hundreds of thousands of Chinamen lost their heads rather than put on the Manchu tail. The Chinese are a peaceable and law-abiding people, and it might be comparatively easy to supplant one dynasty by another; but to attempt to force changes on the people, or to alter their laws and customs, would only make them cling to them the more tenaciously, and retard, rather than hasten, their reformation.

Not enervated by luxury. It is well to note that the more recent history and present habits of the Chinese do not indicate that abandonment to a life of luxury and effeminacy such as has led to the decay and ruin of empires like those of Greece and Rome. It is true they have got far beyond the Emperor who first used *ivory* instead of wooden chopsticks, and was denounced by the *censor* for the ruin of the empire by his indulging in such a luxury. Many of the rich spend large sums on dainty dishes at their feasts, but the people generally are simple and frugal in their habits, and the poor are not kept in idleness and fed on the gifts of wealthy citizens or the *rations* from oppressed provinces, as the Greeks and Romans were before their fall. The worst and most demoralizing vice of this kind is the indulgence in opium-smoking—a vice which has been much increased by the superior quality and scientific preparation of the drug from India, by our own country, and by the wars, which advertized it more effectively than the glaring placards of soaps or pills.

Not to multiply unduly the grounds of our confidence in the future of China, we may group two or three of the more important of them under one general head: the physical, intellectual, and religious characteristics of the people. It is on the constitution and character of a people that we must build our hopes of the stability and progress of a nation.

There are tribes and States in Asia which can boast of a physique superior to that of the Chinese, but they are few in number, and their population is limited. Taken as a whole, in average stature, weight, and muscular strength, there is no large Asiatic population to compare with them. Dr. Wells Williams says: 'Their hands are small and their lower limbs better proportioned than among any Asiatics. The height is about the same as that of Europeans, and a thousand men, taken as they come in the streets of Canton, will probably equal in stature and weight the same number met with in the streets of Rome or New Orleans.' Dr. Williams thinks their muscular power would *probably* be less, but this is, as he admits, doubtful, even among the Cantonese, while in Fuh Kien it would be greater, and in the North of China the stature, weight, and muscle would be decidedly above that of the average European. In face and complexion and colour they are not to be compared æsthetically with the Caucasian type, but physi-

Physical stamina.

cally they will bear favourable comparison with the average specimens of that race.

Intellectual power.

Intellectually, the Chinese take the first place in Asia, for those practical attributes which go to the formation of a skilful mechanic, a steady labourer, an industrious tradesman, an enterprising merchant, an astute statesman, and a peaceful citizen. This is seen in the people of to-day, and is the only way in which we can account for their long and prosperous existence as an empire. We have reason to hope that these useful attributes are a pledge of future progress in the new conditions by which they are environed. Other nations and tribes in Asia excel them in the more ornamental and æsthetic qualities which go to the formation of the artist, the poet, the metaphysician, and all that is attractive and beautiful, in much the same way as the French and other Latin races excel the Saxon race; but it is with those possessed of the more homely and useful qualities that the permanent stability and real progress of empire rests in Asia as in Europe.

Character of their gods.

He was a wise man who said, 'Tell me what their gods are, and I will tell you what the men are.' As another said, 'It is not the gods who have made the men, but the men who have made the gods'; and, as the Scriptures put it, 'Thou thoughtest Me altogether such an one as thyself,' and, 'They that make them are like unto them.' Judged by this test there is no heathen nation, ancient or modern, that can bear comparison with the Chinese, as we have shown in the chapter on religion, which we cannot here repeat. We admit that the superior character of the Supreme God of the Chinese, and the freedom of their inferior deities from the vices which we find in the character of the gods of all other heathen nations, has not saved the Chinese from the practice of vices as gross as those found in other lands; but we are all familiar with the expression, and too often with its practical application, 'Video meliora proboque, deteriora sequor.' But, though we 'follow the worse course,' it is a decided advantage to our moral nature that we do 'see the better and approve it.' It is also a proof of superiority of nature, that we do perceive and admire a moral standard higher than our practice. The superiority of the ideal to the practice of virtue is, of course, a question of degree in different nations, as in individuals. In China it is higher than in any heathen nations of our own, if not of any former age.

That the Chinese presented, as we have seen, a higher and purer conception of God than any other heathen nation is a proof that their moral standard has been higher, though their practice is perhaps as low as that of others. We see this reference to a high standard of moral sentiment in every department of life, from the palace of the Emperor to the hut of the peasant—in Government edicts, in administration of law, in social intercourse, in commercial transactions, and *The standard of morality.*

in the tradesman's shop. All boast of righteousness, justice, charity, truth, and honesty, at the very time when the Government is oppressing the poor, and the judge is accepting a bribe, and the merchant is telling lies to deceive the purchaser, and the tradesman is cheating his customer. This a superficial observer may take as a proof of inferiority, adding hypocrisy to vice. True, the hypocrisy is bad and disgusting, but it is the tribute of vice to virtue, and proves that there is virtue that makes hypocrisy possible and profitable. There is more hypocrisy in Christian than in heathen lands, because there is more virtue to make it worth while to pretend to its possession. In most heathen countries there is little discredit in crimes if not found out, and no shame for vice, because it is the normal state of society. In savage Africa, and in the parts of India in which English education or influence is not felt, or where missionaries have not made their way, the masses of the people have no idea of the moral evil of vice, and commit the most hideous crimes in the name of religion, and with a clear conscience, because their gods are monsters of cruelty and lust. The First Table of the Moral Law does not at once and instinctively commend itself to their reason, and the Second Table receives at best only a qualified approval from their conscience, and many would question its practical application. But read the Ten Commandments to any promiscuous crowd in China,

Is it hypocrisy?

and you will hear a universal expression of approval of each. Even the First Table, asserting the unity of God and the sin of idolatry, will call forth the equivalent words for 'Good,' 'Very good,' and the fifth commandment a universal shout of 'First-rate.'

This enlightenment of conscience, marred though it be by imperfection of faith and violation in practice, has given to Christian missions an advantage in contending against the great difficulties under which they labour in a country like China. China has always shown a readiness to do justice to the teaching of Christianity. In the seventh century it welcomed the Nestorians, and gave every facility for the spread of the Gospel, and the teachers and chapels were reckoned by thousands all over the empire; but they seem to have died out through the corruption of the simplicity of the Gospel, on the one hand, and to depending more on the favour of the Emperor than on the grace of God. They perished through their own unfaithfulness rather than the persecution of the Government. The Roman Catholics, in the end of the sixteenth century, had a most favourable reception, and made great progress, but their own divisions and persecutions among the different *Orders*, and their interference in political affairs, led to their being driven from the country, or into hiding in obscurity, and for centuries they have made little or no progress.

<small>Effect of high moral standard.</small>

Protestant converts.

Protestant missions, though seeking no Court patronage, have made great progress considering the brief period of their existence in the country, the limited number of competent missionaries, the stringency of the conditions of admission into the Church, and the sacrifices the Church members have to make in giving up their most cherished customs, especially ancestor-worship, and often the abandonment of all their earthly possessions, and a life of persecution and suffering, in some cases death itself. Worldly men may make light of the small number of members in the different missions. They overlook the moral and spiritual quality of the converts and the extent of the influence they exert, and forget that the Apostolic missions of the first half-century made about as little impression on the Roman Empire as the Protestant missions of the last fifty years have made on China, if we take into account the much larger population and antiquity of the Chinese Empire. Besides, it was easier to convict the Greek and Roman of the folly of the worship of Zeus or Jupiter than to convince the Chinese of the imperfection of their national worship of Shangti, or Heaven.

It is also worthy of notice that a Chinese convert shows at once a consistency and manliness which we do not find in Hindu converts, whose gods are so vile in character, and the moral standard correspondingly low. Except where they have been brought up under the educational influence of missions or the better class of Government school, even true converts remain feeble, inconsistent, childish, and untrustworthy; while those of China have a moral stamina which gives them stability and character, which can be relied on, and tells on their fellow-countrymen.

A careless reader or a shallow philosopher may turn on us and say there is little hope for an empire of hypocrites, and if they were playing the hypocrite intentionally and universally, or even generally, we would be disposed to agree with them; but the fact is that conscious hypocrisy is not the rule, nor by any means universal. Hypocrisy never is *the rule;* it must be *the exception*, or it would deceive no one; its nature and use are to deceive by imitating or pretending to virtue, admired or followed. It is one thing to have a high standard and come short of it, and quite another thing to use the form of virtue intentionally as a cloak to deceive the virtuous. That there are many of the latter in China we do not doubt, but there are also many who aim at an ideal virtue, though they fail sadly in their efforts to reach the goal, and it is because the Chinese as a people have maintained this high ideal in their conceptions of the nature of God and of the duty of man that we hope for their reformation and progress as an empire.

Characteristics of the People.

Compared with Japanese. Do not let it be supposed that the career of China is over. There is a future for that country which God has so richly stored with all the elements of prosperity in her soil and climate, and so largely blessed in the past. In respect of physical, moral, and intellectual powers, the people are superior to the Japanese. In the movements of Japan and China there is all the difference between the agility of the monkey and the slow and heavy tread of the elephant; but when the elephant does set out on the march its progress will be steady and persevering.

Character of the Chinese. China will not, like Japan, begin its imitation of Western customs by putting on a *tile* hat and a *swallow-tailed* coat—a kind of reform which is apt to be thrown off as quickly as it is put on. China will begin with what is important and useful, and make steady, if slow, progress. Japan's troubles are not over; in fact, they are only beginning. Internal conflicts were staved off by foreign war. That is a game which cannot well be played over again, and unjust wars, like chickens, 'come home to roost.'

We trust to being excused for adding the following estimate of Chinese character from what we wrote thirty years ago, and which we have seen no reason for changing.

The chief faults of the Chinese are a lack of a

sense of honour, cold-blooded cruelty, an inconsistent profession of high-sounding claims to virtue, with the absence of it in practice, and a total disregard of truth. They will tell a dozen lies to cheat one of a farthing. They are licentious, but show a rag of merit left by their attempt to conceal it; the Japanese have thrown away even the rag. Chinese hypocrisy is a small tribute to virtue, and conscience is sufficiently alive to admire the laws of morality, to which their will is too feeble to enforce obedience. There is, however, something to which we can appeal, and convince of sin. In this there is hope.

The Chinese people have elements of character which give the hope of future prosperity for the empire. Their reverence for parents, which has always been the basis of government, gives the best foundation for the preservation of order and subjection to authority. They are peace-loving and easily governed. Their conservatism, if it retards progress, also checks useless innovations, and secures the stability of what progress is gained. They have great reverence for law and order, and have a large fund of common-sense. They are peaceable, industrious, persevering, frugal, and simple in their habits, where they have not been ruined by that vicious indulgence, opium-smoking. They have a genius for trade and commerce, in which no nation excels them but our own, and the race between the two is a keen and close one. In Singapore, that com-

Hope for the future.

mercial navel of the world, where all the nations meet in competition, the Chinese merchant is second to none but the Saxon. The largest fleets of shipping and the handsomest villas, built on the gently-rising knolls around Singapore, often belong to Chinamen. In fact, they are, as we pronounced them forty years ago, THE SAXONS OF ASIA, and no Asiatic people can compete with them. They are far behind us in the awful and questionable accomplishment of the needful art of war, but they are apt scholars under the teaching of good Christian officers. General Gordon wished for no braver and better soldiers than the Chinamen who formed his 'ever-victorious army,' and the same testimony has been borne by many of our British officers. In the late war they were neither drilled, nor clothed, nor armed, nor fed. They had no confidence in their leaders, and the leaders had neither confidence in them nor love for the foreign despot who sent them to fight his quarrels in a hopeless cause. Yet many of them knew how to die at their post like brave men.

Groundless pessimism. The prevalent pessimistic view of the condition and prospects of China is not warranted by her history. The empire is a wonderful unity, notwithstanding its great extent, and has weathered worse storms and come through greater dangers than those which now threaten her. Twenty-six successful rebellions and two foreign conquests left the Chinese Empire unimpaired, and in many cases consolidated and stronger than before; and the last, led by Hung Siu Tsuen, under the title of the Tai Ping Dynasty, had every prospect of driving the Manchu invaders from the throne, until they were attacked and overthrown by the late 'Chinese Gordon,' as he was then called.

No one can suspect the benevolent motives and good intentions of General Gordon in this or in any period of his distinguished career; but that it was a benevolent blunder on the part of that best of men and purest of philanthropists is admitted by the truest friends of China. His frantic attempts, with his own pistol, to shoot Li Hung Chang, by whom he had been employed and duped, was a practical admission that he had made a great mistake, though with his usual facility he soon forgave the duplicity of the man who had deceived him, butchered the Tai Pings and plundered the people. Gordon's aim was to put an end to bloodshed and cruelty; but he found that by defeating the rebels he made way for far greater cruelty and bloodshed by the Imperialists, besides binding a foreign yoke on the necks of the Chinese for at least another generation.

Gordon's mistake.

The leader of the rebels may not have been the man to found a new dynasty, or reform the Government, though the founder of the best and most enduring dynasty in China was, like him, a simple peasant. Hung would have cleared the way for others. He used rough but effectual

Compulsory conversions.

means for putting down opium-smoking; he overthrew idolatry over a large part of China; he put an end to many of the superstitions which now stand in the way of progress; he made a profession of a crude and corrupt form of Christianity, and compelled his followers to adopt it, in much the same way as Constantine imposed it on the Roman Empire, and with far less cruelty than Charlemagne forced it on the Saxons, of whom, in his pious zeal, he slew 4,000 in one day, and with quite as much consistency as St. Olaus, who converted the Scandinavians; while he was equally zealous in proselytism and piracy.

That rebellion, with all its inconsistencies and cruelties, showed that the Chinese mind was capable of freeing itself from its old fetters, and of adopting new and progressive ideas in harmony with the highest form of civilization; and it is to be deplored that that civilization was employed to crush it after it had conquered three-fourths of the empire, and was on the eve of victory over its enemies, the Manchus.

Good out of evil. No Christian of the Apostolic age, or of ours, could recommend or approve of such measures in either Europe or China; but, carried out by men acting up to their imperfect light, they led in Europe to the permanent establishment of Christianity, when followed by the spread of the Scriptures and the teaching of missionaries. In any case, the Chinese rebellion, based on professedly Christian lines, if successful, however imperfect, could not have failed to introduce foreign influences and progressive development, from which confessedly it had received its impulse and power. The leaders had broken with the past by rejecting the works of Confucius as the text-book in all examinations for literary degrees, the key to the highest offices of the State; and by putting the Christian Scriptures in their place they gave a sure pledge of moral and material progress.

I lay no pretensions to prophetic instinct, and make no attempt to foretell the future of China. I aim only at giving the reader materials for forming his own opinions of what China's future may become, in the light of the character and capabilities of the people, their venerable historic antecedents, their admirable self-originated civil institutions, their pure classical literature, their patriarchal religion, and the resources of the country.

The great superiority of the nations by which China has of late been overcome and disorganized lies mainly in mechanical and scientific discoveries of recent years, specially in their application to destructive warfare by Christian nations, who hold the Gospel of peace on earth as a pious theory, and use gunpowder as its practical application. In China the machinery of government has been set up on the theory of their sages, that peace at home is to be preserved by the virtue and beneficence of the rulers, and external conquests to be made by the attractive influence *Adverse theories of government.*

of a well-governed, prosperous, and happy people, to whom strangers, and even enemies, will voluntarily submit, or ally themselves. Hence gunpowder, which they were the first to invent, was only used for firing salutes in honour of friends, and their armies are only a badly disciplined provincial police, neither fitted nor intended for conquest, nor even for national defence. The depravity of rulers — the most of them foreign conquerors — and the cruel and unprepared-for assaults of foreign Powers, have at last opened the eyes of the present generation. Christian nations have convinced the Chinese that human nature is not so good as their old sages had represented it, and that physical, and not moral, forces are necessary for the preservation of peace and of the existence of the empire. This change will not only cause a revulsion in the feelings of the people, it will of itself go far to revolutionize the policy of the Government.

Danger from Russia. The greatest danger which threatens China, and also British commerce and influence in the East, is Russia's getting possession of Manchuria. The Manchus are a bold and warlike race. They have lost much of their sympathy with their countrymen who conquered and settled in China, and still take part in the misgovernment of the country. From the hardy wanderers of the deserts the Russian Government could raise an army which, when disciplined and *stiffened* by a few battalions of Cossacks, could overrun China in the interests of Russia, unless opposed by a larger army of Chinese, drilled, organized, and led by British officers.

This can be done if we show ourselves the true friends of China by standing up for her unity and independence, and showing that we are prepared to stand by her at all risks. Such a policy would prove our highest wisdom, as well as our truest interest, and would be the most likely method for preventing aggression, and preserving peace and prosperity for ourselves and our Chinese allies of the future. Such a policy on the part of Britain would probably lead to Russia contenting herself with the development of the rich and extensive territories she has acquired in the valley of the Amur, and her vast possessions in Siberia, and with the opening up of trade in the East by the extension of her railways, and the possession of a good harbour open at all seasons for her commerce. *Britain's policy.*

Why should Russia be grudged such advantage either in Europe or Asia? For more than thirty years I have held the opinion that it has been both a moral offence and a political folly to oppose the natural aspirations of that growing empire for an outlet to the south in both hemispheres. By shutting her up in her cold and inhospitable northern latitudes, we have made her the hardy, warlike and dangerous power she now is. If Russia had been allowed an outlet to Southern regions a hundred years ago, she would in all *Open ports for Russia.*

probability ere this have been softened and civilized, if not to some extent enervated, by the change of climate and the profitable cultivation of the arts of peace.

There is too great a tendency to regard the Russians as the fierce and implacable enemies of our country and of civilization. If they are, it is because they have been treated as such; it is not because they are naturally cruel or hostile to us. Cruelty is not in general a characteristic of brave and strong people. The highest families of the empire study and admire our language and institutions, and many of them commit their families to the influence of English governesses and tutors. We have good reason to believe that Russia would be ready to co-operate with Britain in preserving the integrity and helping in the development of China if reasonably dealt with; and if these two great empires were agreed on a friendly and fostering policy, no other Power in Europe, Asia, or America would think of interfering with the independence of the Chinese Empire.

APPENDIX.

THE POPULATION OF CHINA.

WE have assumed that the population of China proper is about 400 millions, on the strength of a dissertation on the subject which we appended to our work on 'A Century of Christian Progress,' published ten years ago, when we showed good reason for believing that at that time the population was not less than 380 millions. It is a very moderate increase to take it now at not less than 400 millions.

No Government in the world has shown such care as that of China in taking a census of the population. It is a sacred duty, and forms part of the great annual ritual when the Emperor sacrifices to Shangti. If the returns which are made officially every year show an increase, it is presented to God with joy and thankfulness. If they show a decrease, it is laid before God with profound expressions of sorrow and confession of sin on the part of the ruler.

At the time we wrote we had before us no fewer than seventy of these census returns, showing great variations, which have been taken by many writers as a proof that all were unreliable. But, as we then showed, many of these inconsistencies could be explained by the state of the Empire at the time they were taken, or the object for which they were made at special times.

Some that were very low were accounted for by rebellions at the time, which prevented some provinces being returned. Some that were large were explained by previous periods of unusual peace and prosperity. Some were made as a census of *heads*, with a view to fresh taxes or levies of troops, and, as might be expected in China, means were taken to reduce the numbers returned; others were a census of *mouths* that were to be fed in times of famine, and the numbers were in consequence largely increased.

These irregularities show that the *methods* of taking the annual census were very defective, and the enumerators untrustworthy; but it does not follow that a fairly correct estimate may not be made from the great mass of materials at the disposal of a cautious statistician.

The earliest census that we have seen is that for the second year of the first Christian century, when the population was returned at 12,233,062 families, or 59,504,078 inhabitants. After which the numbers fell much lower, and fluctuated greatly. From the days of Kanghi, who did much to introduce order and uniformity in the method of taking the census, the returns have been much more reliable and consistent, and during the last hundred years, since foreigners have shown an interest in the subject, they seem to be substantially reliable, and where they depart from probability reasons can generally be found for apparent inconsistencies.

The following article from the *North China Herald* of July, 1887, is, we think, conclusive on the subject:

' The results of an examination of these tables*
will be found useful for correcting opinions formed
by many persons, it may be on insufficient data.
The increase during the reign of Taukwang (1821
to 1848) was, according to the annual registration,
71,196,758 ; dividing this by 28, we obtain for the
annual increase 2,542,500. This is 6·3 per cent.
on 400 millions, and it amounts to an increase of
1 person to each group of 157 persons. Malthus
mentions the increase annually in Sweden as 1 to
108, in Russia 1 to 63, in Prussia 1 to 62, in
France 1 to 157, in England 1 to 131. Among
these China most nearly approaches France. At
this rate of increase the population will double
itself in 157 years. But in this case the Chinese
population is increasing at a much slower rate
according to the annual census than in many
European countries. This moderation in the
annual increase is in favour of its being accepted
as not exaggerated, and rather suggests in fact
that the numbers are understated. Malthus found
that the estimate of population for England in
1800 was too little by 1 in 74. The registration
of births was imperfect. Just so it is in China
with the population returns required by law to
be presented annually by local magistrates. It is
the duty of the village bailiff to report the population of his village every spring. If he cannot
write himself, he asks a villager who can do so to
make out the list. The return is sometimes under
the truth, through the desire felt by the fathers of
grown-up sons to save them from conscription.
Only persons at home are counted, but occasionally when some visitor is expected he is counted
in, in order that suspicion may not fall on him as

* Of the elaborate tables we need give only one, as a
sample of the result of a Chinese census.

an unregistered person when he arrives. The reasons for understating the number of a household are, however, much stronger than those for overstating it, and are much more widely influential. The people in a locality are often not counted again for many years in succession, the old lists being used.

'When Père Allerstain was President of the Board of Astronomy in 1760, he obtained the census from the Board of Revenue, and it gave 197 millions as the population of China for that year. The next year it was more than 198 millions. During the sixty years that elapsed from that time to the reign of Taukwang the population rose to 355 millions. The increase was 157 millions, and was made up of annual additions of about 2½ millions — the same as in the period from 1820 to 1848. Knowing this fact, we feel confidence in the correctness of the returns. The causes of increase are always at work — the thoroughness of the agriculture, the fertility of the soil, the anxiety of parents to see their sons married by the time they are eighteen, the willingness of the women to be married at seventeen or thereabouts, and become domestic drudges in their husband's home for the first few years of married life; the equality of sons as heirs to property, the thrifty habits of the people, and their adaptability to a variety of occupations requiring skill and industry. Yet with these powerful causes operating, the census is augmented at quite a moderate pace. Amyot, Malthus, Williams, accept and vindicate the Chinese numbers. It is just as well for us to follow these good examples of sober judgment on the part of men who have studied the subject. It is worth remarking that Amyot was astonished at the rapid increase of

Appendix

population which he noticed in Szechuen, which had risen from 144,000 families, liable to the population tax, to 3,036,342. He adds, "this prodigious augmentation comes no doubt from the presence of refugees who sought a new home there at the time of the Manchu conquest." He did not think that the census would a century later represent the population of Szechuen as 71 millions. Yet so it is. We must now be prepared for the unexpected conclusion that the provinces are none of them populated up to the point when the fertility of the soil cannot maintain the inhabitants. When drought and war occur, the people fly to the next province, the provinces take their turns in being thickly or thinly populated, and with new aids against famines and civil war they might, it would seem, support 800 millions without much difficulty. If this were the case, Kiangsu need not be more thickly peopled than it was forty years ago, and intelligent foreign travellers would scarcely notice the difference. The census returns for each year are imperfect: they are probably not really new in a multitude of cases. But when the people are counted it is done with as much accuracy as possible, and the amount is under the actual population.'

TABLE OF POPULATION OF CHINA, DRAWN UP BY
MR. POPOFF FROM OFFICIAL DOCUMENTS OF THE
YEAR 1882, SUPPLEMENTED WHERE DEFECTIVE BY
THOSE OF 1879.

Provinces.	Population, 1842.	Population, 1882.	Gain and Loss.	English Square Miles.	Population in a Square Mile.
Shantung	29,529,877	36,247,835	+ 6,717,958	65,104	557
Shansi	17,096,925	12,211,453	− 4,845,472	56,268	221
Honan	29,069,771	22,115,827	− 6,953,941	65,104	340
Kiangsu	39,646,924	20,905,171	−18,741,753	44,500	470
Kiangsi	26,513,889	24,534,118	− 1,979,771	72,176	340
Chekiang	30,437,974	11,588,692	−18,849,282	39,150	296
Hupei	28,584,564	33,365,005	+ 4,780,441	70,650	473
Hunan	20,048,969	21,002,604	+ 953,635	74,320	822
Szechuen	22,256,964	67,712,897	+45,455,933	166,800	406
Kuangtung	21,152,603	29,706,249	+ 8,553,646	79,456	377
		279,389,885			

Provinces.	Census of Year 1842.	Population in Year 1879.	Gain and Loss.	English Square Miles.	Population in a Square Mile.
Yünnan	5,823,670	11,721,576	+ 5,897,906	107,969	108
Kueichow	5,679,128	7,669,181	+ 1,990,053	64,554	118
Shensi	10,309,769	8,432,193	− 1,877,576	67,400	126
Kansu	19,512,716	5,411,188	−14,101,528	86,608	62
Chili	36,879,838	17,937,000	−18,942,838	58,949	304
		51,171,138			
Anhwei	36,596,988	20,596,988	−16,000,000	48,461	425
Kuangsi	8,121,327	5,121,327	− 3,000,000	78,250	65
Fukien	25,799,556	25,799,556	...	53,480	482
	413,021,452	382,078,860	−30,942,592	1,297,999	234

The fall from 415 millions in 1842 to 382 millions in 1882 is quite what one might expect, from what was suffered from the great wars of the Tai Ping rebellion and the massacres and oppression of those who crushed it; and if it was 382 millions in 1882, it cannot be less than 400 millions in 1898.

INDEX.

ADMINISTRATION, 85
Agnostic school of criticism, 103
Agriculture honourable, 40
Army, The, how controlled, 84
Autocratic government, 81; limitations of, 82

Books, The sacred or classical, 101, 104; the four, 107
Boswell, The Chinese, 119
Britain's policy, 171; duty, viii

Canal, The Great, 24, 76
Chesterfield, A Chinese, 49
Chi, the Napoleon of China, 64
Children, 59; education of, 60; filial affection of, 59
China, 1, 4; absence of monuments in, 21; ancient description of, 3; future of, 81 (see Future); fauna of, 17; flora of, 13; Great Wall of, 23; lakes and lake poets, 10; mineral resources of, 19; name of, 2; physical features of, 7
Chinese, Civilization of the, 67; character of their gods, 139, 146, 148; converts to Christianity, 162; habits and manners of, 46; industries, early, 32; mental qualities, 29, 158, 165; moral character of, 159, 164; physical standard, 27, 157; trade and commerce of, 37, 165; women, 51
Chinese empire, antiquity of, 63, 68; decadence of, 78; disasters, 89; history of, 62, 67; rebellions frequent, 64
Christianity, influence of, 80
Cities of China, 39
Civil power and honour the highest, 88
Civilization, 32, 35, 46

Coal abundant, 19
Commercial enterprise, 165
Confucius, Appearance of, 106; his influence, 105, 107; not founder of a religion, 128; sacred canon fixed by, 137; sayings of, 120; work of, 104, 129
Criminal code, The, 85
Cyclopedias, 123

Decadence, causes of, 78
Degrees, examinations for, 92; military titles inferior to civil, 93
Dictionaries, 123
Divorce, 54
Dynasties from 2200 B.C., 71

Education, 92; of children, 60
Emperor as the only priest of the empire, 141
Examinations for degrees, 93

Farming, 42
Fauna of China, 17
Filial obedience, 59
Flora of China, 13
Forms of civility morally significant, 50
Four Books, The, 118
Fuh hi, 62
Future of China, 81; hopeful signs, 159; hopeful awaking, 151, 153; hope in character of people, 164; in light of history, 155

Garden of Sse Ma Kouang, 10
God, Attributes of, 140, 158; odes to, 115, 117; prayer to, 145
Gordon, General, Great mistake of,'167
Government, 81, 169; by moral force, 87; examinations for appointments, 39

Habits and customs, 46
' Happy though married,' 56
Henotheists, not Monotheists, 139
Historical faculty of the Chinese, 62
History of the empire, 62, 130
Hymns, 146
Hypocrisy, 163

Industries fossilized, 44
Invasions, not revolutions, 65

Japanese war: victory, not conquest, 87; victories, how obtained, 90, 152

Kublai Khan, 75

Lakes and lake poets, 10
Land, Price of, 41; revenue from, 43; tenure of, 40
Language as spoken and written, 99
Laotsze, a religious mystic, 132
Laws, Code of, 85
Letters, Early, 95; inconvenience of, 97
Libraries, 121
Li Ki, The, 118
Limitations on autocracy, 82
Literature, 101; general, 121; 'Augustan Age' of, 124

Manchu invasion, 77
Manners of Chinese, 49
Manufactures, Ancient, 35
Marriage, 53; customs, 55
Mencius' mother, 52
Mineral resources, 19
Mongolian invasion, 65
Monuments, Absence of, 21
Moral standard of the Chinese, 159, 161
Moral influence as governing power, 87
Mothers honoured, 112

Odes, 111
Origin of the empire, 66

Patriarchal government, 81
Peking Gazette, 84
Philosophy, 75
Physical geography, 7; its influences on religion, 25
Poetry, Chinese estimates of, 110, 124
Polygamy, 53, 113
Population, 5, and Appendix
Prayer by the Emperor, 145
Priest — the Emperor priest of empire, 141
Printing, Discovery of art of, 74

Rebellion, Right of, 83. 88
Rebellions many, one revolution, 64
Religion, 127, 130; henotheism, 139; of Laotsze, 132; past and present, 131; patriarchal, 137; pure, 148; revival of sixth century B.C. 128
Religious sacrifice, 123
Russians, Danger from, 170; and open ports, 171

Sacred books, The, 101
Sacrifices, 123
Shi King, 109; odes of, 111
Shoo King 107
Shun, 67

Tai Ping rebellion, 166; arrested by General Gordon, 167; what it might have done, 168
Tolerance of Chinese, 138; false and true, 139
Tones in Chinese, 98

Wall, The Great, 23
Wives, 116
Woman's position, 51, 112
Worship, Forms of, 143
Writing, Origin of, 96

Yao and Shun, 67
Yih King, 117
Yu, The engineer and emperor, 17, 108

Elliot Stock, 62, Paternoster Row, London.

www.ingramcontent.com/pod-product-compliance
Lightning Source LLC
Chambersburg PA
CBHW032139160426
43197CB00008B/710